CRM and SRM Mastery:

A Guide for Industry Professionals

Table of Contents

Part 1: Foundations of CRM and SRM _____ 5

1. Introduction to CRM and SRM: Definitions, Evolution, and Strategic Importance _____ 6

2. The Relationship Economy: Why Relationships Drive Modern Business Success _____ 12

3. Key Differences and Synergies: CRM vs. SRM, and Where They Intersect _____ 17

4. The Role of Technology in Relationship Management: Tools and Platforms _____ 24

5. Core Principles of Effective Relationship Management: Trust, Communication, and Collaboration _____ 30

Part 2: Building a Customer-Centric CRM System _____ 37

6. Understanding Customer Needs: Insights Through Data and Feedback _____ 38

CRM Tools and Platforms: Choosing the Right Solution for Your Business _____ 48

8. Personalization in CRM: Leveraging Data for Tailored Experiences _____ 55

9. Automation in CRM: Streamlining Processes with Technology _____ 62

10. Measuring CRM Success: Key Performance Indicators (KPIs) and Metrics _____ 70

Part 3: Optimizing Supplier Relationships with SRM _____ 78

11. Supplier Segmentation and Evaluation: Identifying Strategic Partners _____ 79

12. Building Supplier Partnerships: Collaboration for Innovation and Growth _____ 86

13. Technology in SRM: From e-Procurement to Blockchain Applications _____ 93

14. Managing Supplier Risks: Mitigating Disruptions in the Supply Chain _____ 100

15. Sustainability in SRM: Promoting Ethical and Green Supply Chains _____ 108

Part 4: Integrating CRM and SRM for Holistic Success _____ 115

16. Unified Relationship Management: Bridging the Customer and Supplier Divide _____ 116

17. Data Integration Across CRM and SRM: Creating a Seamless Flow of Information _____ 123

18. Shared Metrics and Analytics: Measuring ROI on Relationships _____ 131

19. Overcoming Integration Challenges: Aligning Processes, Tools, and Culture _____ 138

20. Collaborative Case Studies: Examples of Successful CRM-SRM Integration _____ 145

21. AI and Machine Learning in CRM and SRM: Enhancing Decision-Making and Predictions _____ 153

22. The Role of Big Data: Driving Insights for Customer and Supplier Strategies _____ 160

23. Global Trends in CRM and SRM: Adapting to an Interconnected World _____ 167

24. Preparing for the Future: Agility and Innovation in Relationship Management _____ *174*

*25. Key Takeaways and Action Plan: Building a Sustainable Relationship Strategy*_____ *181*

Part 1: Foundations of CRM and SRM

1. Introduction to CRM and SRM: Definitions, Evolution, and Strategic Importance

Customer Relationship Management (CRM) and Supplier Relationship Management (SRM) have emerged as pivotal frameworks in modern business operations, reshaping how organizations interact with their key stakeholders. These concepts are not merely operational tools but strategic imperatives that drive value, foster innovation, and sustain competitive advantages in dynamic markets. Understanding the essence of CRM and SRM, their evolution, and their strategic importance requires a deep dive into their definitions, historical context, and their transformative roles in shaping contemporary business landscapes.

At its core, Customer Relationship Management refers to the methodologies, technologies, and strategies employed by organizations to manage and analyze customer interactions throughout the lifecycle of the relationship. It encompasses a suite of practices designed to enhance customer retention, optimize customer satisfaction, and ultimately drive sales growth. CRM is as much a philosophy as it is a toolset; it represents an organizational commitment to prioritizing customer needs and leveraging insights derived from data to create meaningful, personalized experiences. CRM systems, often powered by advanced technologies such as artificial intelligence and analytics, serve as the backbone of this philosophy, offering actionable intelligence that informs marketing, sales, and service strategies.

In parallel, Supplier Relationship Management focuses on the systematic engagement with suppliers to maximize the value derived from these critical partnerships. Unlike CRM, which is customer-facing, SRM addresses the supply side of business operations, emphasizing collaboration, risk mitigation, and value creation. It involves segmenting suppliers based on their strategic importance, fostering long-term partnerships with key vendors, and utilizing technology to streamline procurement and communication processes. SRM is more than procurement; it is a strategic approach to managing supply networks, enabling businesses to innovate, reduce costs, and respond effectively to market disruptions.

The evolution of CRM and SRM is deeply intertwined with the broader narrative of technological advancement and globalization. Historically, customer and supplier relationships were managed through manual processes, limited by the constraints of physical proximity and the absence of digital tools. The industrial era marked the beginning of structured relationship management, with businesses leveraging standardized practices to manage their supply chains and customer bases. However, these practices were often transactional, focused on efficiency and cost rather than strategic value.

The advent of computing in the latter half of the 20th century revolutionized relationship management. Early CRM systems emerged as database tools to store customer information, while SRM frameworks evolved from traditional procurement practices into more sophisticated supply chain management systems. The integration of Enterprise Resource Planning (ERP) systems in the 1990s further bridged the gap between operational and strategic relationship management, enabling organizations to manage resources, suppliers, and customer interactions more cohesively.

In the 21st century, the rise of the internet, mobile technologies, and big data has exponentially expanded the capabilities of CRM and SRM. CRM platforms have evolved into multifaceted ecosystems incorporating customer

data from diverse touchpoints, such as social media, email campaigns, website interactions, and customer service engagements. This transformation has allowed organizations to adopt a more holistic view of their customers, predicting their needs and behaviors with greater accuracy. Modern CRM systems not only track historical interactions but also enable real-time engagement through personalized content, offers, and communication. These advancements underline the strategic shift from reactive customer service to proactive customer experience management.

Similarly, SRM has transitioned from a cost-reduction and procurement-focused model to a comprehensive approach that emphasizes strategic partnerships and innovation. Today's SRM systems integrate advanced analytics, predictive modeling, and collaboration platforms to enhance supplier evaluation, risk assessment, and performance management. These tools empower businesses to anticipate potential disruptions, such as those caused by geopolitical uncertainties or global pandemics, and to create resilient supply chains that can adapt to rapidly changing circumstances. SRM now stands as a critical pillar in ensuring business continuity and achieving competitive differentiation in global markets.

The strategic importance of CRM and SRM lies in their ability to align business operations with overarching organizational goals. CRM focuses on driving top-line growth by enhancing customer loyalty and satisfaction, while SRM contributes to bottom-line efficiency through cost management and value co-creation with suppliers. Together, these frameworks form the bedrock of sustainable business success by fostering interconnected ecosystems of trust, collaboration, and innovation.

From a strategic perspective, CRM enables businesses to leverage customer insights to develop targeted marketing strategies, tailor product offerings, and refine service delivery. It also supports data-driven decision-making, ensuring that organizational resources are allocated effectively to meet customer expectations. For instance, a well-implemented CRM system can help a company identify its most profitable customer segments and focus its efforts on nurturing these relationships. This not only increases customer lifetime value but also optimizes marketing spend and resource utilization.

On the other hand, SRM plays a critical role in risk management and operational efficiency. By segmenting suppliers based on their strategic importance, organizations can prioritize their engagement with key vendors, ensuring that critical supplies are always available. Strategic SRM practices, such as joint innovation initiatives and collaborative planning, can also unlock new opportunities for growth and differentiation. For example, a technology company might collaborate with its suppliers to co-develop innovative components, giving it a competitive edge in the marketplace.

Furthermore, the integration of CRM and SRM offers unparalleled opportunities for businesses to create synergies across their value chains. For example, insights derived from CRM can inform procurement decisions, ensuring that suppliers are aligned with customer preferences and market demands. Similarly, data from SRM can enhance CRM strategies by ensuring that products and services meet quality and sustainability standards valued by customers. This interconnected approach not only drives efficiency but also fosters a cohesive brand identity that resonates with stakeholders.

The evolution of CRM and SRM also reflects the growing emphasis on sustainability and corporate social responsibility. As customers and regulators demand greater transparency and accountability, businesses are leveraging CRM and SRM systems to meet these expectations. CRM platforms now include features for tracking and communicating sustainability initiatives to customers, while SRM systems help organizations evaluate the environmental and ethical practices of their suppliers. This alignment with sustainability goals not only enhances brand reputation but also mitigates risks associated with non-compliance and reputational damage.

In today's digital age, the boundaries between CRM and SRM are increasingly blurred as organizations adopt integrated platforms that span the entire value chain. Cloud-based solutions, artificial intelligence, and Internet of Things (IoT) technologies are driving this convergence, enabling real-time data sharing and collaboration across customer and supplier ecosystems. For instance, a manufacturing firm might use an integrated CRM-SRM platform to synchronize its demand forecasts with supplier production schedules, ensuring timely delivery of products while minimizing inventory costs.

However, the successful implementation of CRM and SRM systems requires more than just technological investment. It demands a cultural shift within organizations, where relationship management is viewed as a shared responsibility across departments. Sales, marketing, procurement, and operations teams must work collaboratively to ensure that customer and supplier relationships are managed effectively. Leadership commitment and cross-functional alignment are critical to realizing the full potential of these frameworks.

In conclusion, CRM and SRM are not just operational tools but strategic enablers that empower organizations to thrive in complex and competitive environments. By fostering stronger relationships with customers and suppliers, businesses can drive innovation, enhance efficiency, and achieve sustainable growth. As the landscape continues to evolve, the integration of CRM and SRM will become increasingly central to organizational success, providing a foundation for building resilient and adaptive business ecosystems. Understanding their definitions, historical evolution, and strategic importance is the first step for professionals aiming to harness their transformative potential.

2. The Relationship Economy: Why Relationships Drive Modern Business Success

In today's hyper-connected and competitive landscape, the concept of the relationship economy underscores the pivotal role that meaningful connections play in driving business success. Unlike traditional economies that relied heavily on tangible assets and transactional exchanges, the relationship economy emphasizes trust, collaboration, and value co-creation. Organizations that excel in building and maintaining strong relationships with their customers, suppliers, and stakeholders are better positioned to adapt to changing market dynamics, foster loyalty, and sustain long-term growth. Understanding why relationships drive modern business success requires a deep exploration of the evolving business environment, the rise of connectivity, and the strategic advantages of relationship-based management.

The emergence of the relationship economy is rooted in a fundamental shift in how value is created and exchanged. Historically, businesses operated in a product-centric environment where the quality and cost of goods and services were the primary drivers of success. Relationships were often secondary to transactional efficiency, with companies prioritizing production, logistics, and price competition. However, the advent of globalization and digital transformation has significantly altered this paradigm. In an era characterized by abundant choices, customer empowerment, and rapid technological innovation, relationships have become the cornerstone of differentiation.

At its core, the relationship economy recognizes that trust and emotional connection are critical to building customer and supplier loyalty. Customers today are not merely seeking products or services; they are looking for experiences, values, and alignment with brands they trust. Similarly, suppliers are no longer seen merely as providers but as strategic partners who can contribute to innovation and operational excellence. In this context, businesses that cultivate deep, authentic relationships gain a competitive edge by creating ecosystems where mutual value is exchanged and sustained over time.

Technology has been a catalyst for the relationship economy, transforming how businesses interact with their stakeholders. Customer Relationship Management (CRM) systems, for example, enable organizations to collect, analyze, and leverage vast amounts of data to create personalized experiences. By understanding individual preferences, behaviors, and feedback, businesses can anticipate customer needs and deliver solutions that resonate on a personal level. Similarly, Supplier Relationship Management (SRM) tools allow businesses to assess supplier performance, streamline communication, and foster collaboration. These technologies not only enhance operational efficiency but also build the trust and transparency necessary for enduring partnerships.

Another hallmark of the relationship economy is the emphasis on long-term value over short-term gains. In traditional transactional models, the focus was often on immediate profitability and cost savings. However, the relationship-driven approach prioritizes the lifetime value of a customer or supplier. For instance, a loyal customer who repeatedly engages with a brand provides greater financial and reputational benefits than one who makes a single purchase. Similarly, a trusted supplier who consistently delivers high-quality materials or collaborates on innovation projects contributes more strategically to an organization's success than a low-cost alternative that lacks reliability.

This shift toward relationship-centric strategies is particularly evident in the way organizations approach customer engagement. Modern businesses employ omni-channel communication strategies, utilizing platforms such as social media, email, chatbots, and in-person interactions to maintain constant and meaningful dialogue with their customers. This ensures that customers feel valued and heard, even in highly competitive markets. Personalized marketing campaigns, loyalty programs, and customer support tailored to individual preferences are some of the tactics that exemplify the relationship economy in action.

Supplier engagement has also evolved in the relationship economy. Organizations are moving away from adversarial procurement practices toward collaborative partnerships that prioritize mutual success. For example, many companies now involve their key suppliers in product development processes, leveraging their expertise and insights to create innovative solutions. Such collaborative approaches not only enhance product quality but also strengthen the bonds between businesses and their suppliers, fostering loyalty and shared success.

The relationship economy also extends beyond customers and suppliers to include a broader network of stakeholders. Employees, investors, communities, and even competitors are part of the interconnected ecosystems that define modern businesses. For instance, fostering a strong organizational culture and employee engagement is essential for delivering consistent and authentic customer experiences. Similarly, maintaining transparent and ethical relationships with investors and regulatory bodies helps build trust and credibility in the market.

In addition to fostering loyalty and collaboration, relationships drive modern business success by mitigating risks and enhancing adaptability. In a volatile and uncertain world, businesses that have strong relationships with their stakeholders are better equipped to navigate challenges such as supply chain disruptions, economic downturns, or shifts in consumer preferences. For example, during the COVID-19 pandemic, organizations with robust supplier relationships were able to secure critical materials and maintain operations more effectively than those with transactional, cost-focused supplier networks.

The strategic importance of the relationship economy is further amplified by its alignment with contemporary consumer values. Today's customers and stakeholders are increasingly drawn to organizations that demonstrate social and environmental responsibility. By building relationships based on shared values, businesses can strengthen their brand reputation and create loyal communities of advocates. This is particularly important in an age where social media amplifies the voices of consumers and stakeholders, making it essential for organizations to align their actions with their stated values.

The benefits of the relationship economy are clear, but achieving success in this paradigm requires a deliberate and strategic approach. Building strong relationships demands consistent effort, open communication, and a willingness to invest in long-term outcomes. Businesses must adopt a mindset that prioritizes empathy, adaptability, and value creation, viewing their stakeholders not as mere counterparts but as integral partners in a shared journey toward success.

In conclusion, the relationship economy underscores the importance of trust, collaboration, and mutual value creation in driving modern business success. As businesses navigate an increasingly complex and competitive environment, the ability to build and sustain meaningful relationships with customers, suppliers, and other stakeholders will remain a critical determinant of success. By embracing the principles of the relationship economy, organizations can create resilient ecosystems that not only withstand challenges but also thrive in an interconnected and rapidly evolving world.

3.Key Differences and Synergies: CRM vs. SRM, and Where They Intersect

Understanding CRM and SRM in Business Contexts

Customer Relationship Management (CRM) and Supplier Relationship Management (SRM) are two pivotal frameworks that underpin modern business operations. While they cater to distinct segments of an organization's ecosystem, they share common principles and, when effectively integrated, can generate substantial synergies. CRM is primarily focused on managing relationships with customers, aiming to enhance satisfaction, loyalty, and revenue generation. SRM, on the other hand, is concerned with building and maintaining productive partnerships with suppliers, emphasizing efficiency, risk management, and value co-creation.

Though CRM and SRM serve different purposes, they operate on the foundational principle of relationship management, which highlights the importance of trust, collaboration, and mutual benefit. By exploring the key differences and synergies between these systems, as well as their points of intersection, organizations can unlock new opportunities for competitive advantage and operational excellence.

The Core Objectives of CRM

CRM systems are designed to optimize interactions between a business and its customers. Their primary objectives include understanding customer needs, predicting behaviors, personalizing engagement, and improving satisfaction. The insights derived from CRM data allow organizations to develop targeted marketing strategies, refine product offerings, and deliver superior service. CRM enables businesses to view their customers holistically, tracking their journey from initial contact to post-sale support.

At the heart of CRM is the goal of fostering loyalty. In competitive markets where customer acquisition costs are high, retaining existing customers is critical. CRM platforms facilitate this by enabling personalized communication, identifying opportunities for cross-selling or upselling, and addressing customer concerns proactively. Additionally, CRM tools often integrate with sales and marketing systems, creating a seamless flow of information that enhances decision-making and ensures a consistent customer experience.

The Core Objectives of SRM

In contrast, SRM focuses on the organization's supply-side relationships. Its core objectives include ensuring the reliability of supply chains, optimizing procurement costs, driving innovation through collaboration, and mitigating risks. SRM systems provide tools for evaluating supplier performance, monitoring compliance, and streamlining communication.

A robust SRM framework segments suppliers based on their strategic importance, allowing businesses to allocate resources and attention accordingly. For example, critical suppliers that provide unique components or services are managed differently from commodity suppliers where cost considerations dominate. By fostering long-term partnerships with key suppliers, organizations can co-develop solutions, enhance quality, and achieve sustainability goals.

Another key aspect of SRM is risk management. In today's globalized markets, supply chain disruptions—whether caused by natural disasters, geopolitical tensions, or economic volatility—pose significant risks. SRM tools enable businesses to identify potential vulnerabilities and develop contingency plans, ensuring resilience and continuity.

Key Differences Between CRM and SRM

While CRM and SRM share the overarching goal of optimizing relationships, their focus areas and operational dynamics differ significantly.

CRM is inherently customer-facing, with an outward focus on the end-user of a product or service. It deals with understanding consumer behavior, preferences, and purchasing patterns to enhance engagement. Conversely, SRM has an inward operational focus, managing relationships with entities that provide goods and services necessary for business operations.

The metrics used to measure success also differ. In CRM, key performance indicators (KPIs) often revolve around customer satisfaction, retention rates, average order value, and net promoter scores. In SRM, KPIs are more likely to include supplier performance, on-time delivery rates, procurement cost savings, and supplier risk assessments.

Technology applications reflect these differences as well. CRM systems are typically equipped with features like customer segmentation, marketing automation, and sales forecasting. In contrast, SRM systems prioritize capabilities such as supplier scorecards, contract management, and procurement analytics.

Another critical distinction lies in the emotional component of the relationships. Customer relationships often have a strong emotional aspect, as brands aim to build trust and loyalty through personalized experiences. Supplier relationships, while collaborative, are more transactional and performance-driven, emphasizing reliability, cost-efficiency, and compliance.

Synergies Between CRM and SRM

Despite their differences, CRM and SRM are deeply interconnected and can create powerful synergies when integrated effectively. This integration is particularly evident in industries where customer preferences influence supply chain dynamics, such as retail, manufacturing, and technology.

One significant area of synergy is data integration. By combining insights from CRM and SRM systems, businesses can align their customer-facing and supplier-facing operations. For example, demand forecasts generated by CRM systems can inform supplier planning and inventory management, ensuring that supply chains are agile and responsive to market needs. Similarly, supplier performance data from SRM systems can help organizations deliver consistent product quality and meet customer expectations.

Another synergy lies in the alignment of organizational goals. Both CRM and SRM contribute to achieving business objectives such as revenue growth, cost optimization, and risk mitigation. For instance, a company focused on sustainability can leverage CRM to communicate its green initiatives to customers while using SRM to source environmentally friendly materials. This alignment not only strengthens brand reputation but also enhances stakeholder trust and loyalty.

Collaboration across CRM and SRM teams can also drive innovation. When customer feedback from CRM is shared with suppliers via SRM, it creates opportunities for co-development and product improvement. For example, a technology company might relay user insights about product design to its suppliers, enabling the creation of next-generation components that meet customer needs more effectively.

Points of Intersection

The intersection of CRM and SRM is most evident in the context of the value chain, where customer demand drives supply chain activities. This interdependence underscores the importance of a unified approach to relationship management.

One critical intersection is demand planning. Accurate demand forecasts generated by CRM systems are essential for effective procurement and production planning in SRM. A disconnect between these functions can result in overstocking, stockouts, or delays, all of which negatively impact customer satisfaction and operational efficiency.

Another point of intersection is quality management. While CRM focuses on ensuring that customers receive high-quality products and services, SRM plays a crucial role in securing quality inputs from suppliers. By aligning quality standards and expectations across CRM and SRM, organizations can deliver consistent value to customers.

Technology integration is another area where CRM and SRM intersect. Modern enterprise resource planning (ERP) systems often include modules for both CRM and SRM, enabling seamless data flow and coordination between customer-facing and supplier-facing operations. For instance, a unified platform might allow sales teams to view supplier lead times, enabling more accurate delivery commitments to customers.

Strategic Benefits of Integrating CRM and SRM

The integration of CRM and SRM offers numerous strategic benefits. It enhances visibility across the value chain, enabling organizations to identify inefficiencies and opportunities for improvement. It also fosters collaboration, both internally and externally, by breaking down silos between customer and supplier functions.

Moreover, integration supports a customer-centric approach to supply chain management. By aligning supplier activities with customer needs, organizations can create a more agile and responsive value chain. This is particularly important in industries where customer preferences change rapidly, such as fashion, electronics, and consumer goods.

The Future of CRM and SRM Integration

As digital transformation continues to reshape business landscapes, the convergence of CRM and SRM is likely to deepen. Emerging technologies such as artificial intelligence, blockchain, and IoT are driving new opportunities for integration and collaboration. For example, AI-powered analytics can provide real-time insights into customer demand and supplier performance, enabling more proactive decision-making.

Blockchain technology can enhance transparency and trust across CRM and SRM systems by providing a secure, immutable record of transactions and interactions. Similarly, IoT devices can facilitate real-time communication and coordination between customers, suppliers, and businesses, creating a more connected and efficient ecosystem.

In conclusion, CRM and SRM are distinct yet complementary frameworks that play a crucial role in modern business success. By understanding their differences, leveraging their synergies, and identifying points of intersection, organizations can create integrated strategies that drive value across the entire value chain. The strategic alignment of CRM and SRM not only enhances operational efficiency but also strengthens relationships, fosters innovation, and ensures sustainable growth in an increasingly interconnected world.

4.The Role of Technology in Relationship Management: Tools and Platforms

In the contemporary business landscape, technology is not merely an enabler; it is the backbone of effective relationship management. Whether managing customers or suppliers, technology-driven tools and platforms provide organizations with the capabilities to streamline processes, enhance engagement, and make data-driven decisions. As businesses face increasingly complex challenges—ranging from customer expectations for personalized experiences to the need for resilient supply chains—technological advancements are transforming how relationships are built, nurtured, and optimized.

The Technological Evolution in Relationship Management

The evolution of relationship management technology reflects broader changes in business practices and customer behavior. In the early stages, organizations relied on rudimentary methods, such as spreadsheets and manual data entry, to track interactions. These methods, though functional, were labor-intensive and prone to errors, limiting scalability and accuracy.

With the advent of the digital age, Customer Relationship Management (CRM) and Supplier Relationship Management (SRM) systems emerged as essential tools for managing relationships more effectively. These systems are now central to relationship management strategies, offering advanced functionalities like real-time data analytics, automated workflows, and integration capabilities. As the complexity of relationships has grown, so too have the demands on these tools, leading to innovations that harness artificial intelligence, machine learning, blockchain, and the Internet of Things (IoT).

CRM Tools and Platforms: Enhancing Customer Connections

CRM platforms are designed to centralize and analyze customer data, enabling businesses to engage with their customers in a more meaningful and targeted manner. These tools facilitate a range of activities, from sales and marketing to customer service and retention.

Some of the most prominent CRM tools include Salesforce, HubSpot, Microsoft Dynamics 365, and Zoho CRM.

One of the defining features of modern CRM platforms is their ability to provide a 360-degree view of the customer. By aggregating data from various touchpoints—such as website interactions, social media engagement, and purchase history—CRMs allow businesses to gain deeper insights into customer preferences and behavior. This enables personalized communication, which is critical for building trust and loyalty.

Automation is another powerful feature of CRM tools. From sending automated email campaigns to assigning leads to sales representatives, automation reduces manual effort and ensures consistency in customer interactions. Moreover, AI-powered CRMs can analyze customer sentiment, predict buying patterns, and even recommend next-best actions for sales teams.

In the realm of customer support, CRM platforms integrate seamlessly with helpdesk software and chatbots, enabling businesses to resolve issues quickly and efficiently. Customers now expect instant responses and solutions, and CRM technology plays a pivotal role in meeting these expectations.

SRM Tools and Platforms: Strengthening Supplier Partnerships

On the supply side, SRM tools are instrumental in managing supplier relationships and ensuring that procurement processes align with organizational goals. Popular SRM platforms include SAP Ariba, Coupa, Oracle Procurement Cloud, and Jaggaer.

SRM platforms focus on supplier evaluation, performance monitoring, and collaboration. These tools allow businesses to segment their suppliers based on criteria such as strategic importance, cost, and risk. By providing a clear picture of supplier performance through scorecards and dashboards, SRM systems enable organizations to make informed decisions about contract renewals, supplier development programs, and risk mitigation strategies.

Collaboration is a key feature of SRM tools. Many platforms offer integrated communication channels, document sharing, and joint project management functionalities. For example, businesses and suppliers can co-develop new products or address quality issues through shared digital workspaces. This fosters a sense of partnership rather than a transactional relationship.

Procurement analytics is another critical component of SRM platforms. By analyzing data on spending patterns, contract compliance, and supplier diversity, businesses can identify cost-saving opportunities, improve procurement efficiency, and align their supply chain practices with sustainability goals.

Integration of CRM and SRM Systems

While CRM and SRM tools operate in distinct domains, integrating them can unlock significant value. For instance, when customer demand data from CRM systems informs supplier planning in SRM platforms, businesses can create more responsive and agile supply chains. Similarly, insights from supplier performance data can help ensure consistent product quality and timely deliveries, enhancing the customer experience.

Integrated systems often rely on enterprise resource planning (ERP) platforms, which provide a unified interface for managing both customer and supplier data. ERP solutions like SAP, Oracle, and Microsoft Dynamics offer modules for CRM and SRM, enabling seamless data flow and cross-functional collaboration.

Emerging Technologies in Relationship Management

The rapid pace of technological innovation is driving new possibilities for relationship management. Emerging technologies are enhancing the capabilities of traditional CRM and SRM tools, making them more intelligent, interconnected, and user-centric.

Artificial Intelligence (AI) and Machine Learning (ML) are transforming how businesses analyze and act on data. In CRM, AI can provide predictive insights into customer behavior, automate lead scoring, and deliver hyper-personalized recommendations. In SRM, AI can forecast supply chain disruptions, identify cost-saving opportunities, and optimize procurement strategies.

Blockchain technology is enhancing transparency and trust in relationships. For instance, blockchain-enabled CRMs can provide customers with verifiable information about product origins, supporting ethical sourcing initiatives. In SRM, blockchain facilitates secure and tamper-proof transactions, reducing fraud and ensuring compliance.

The Internet of Things (IoT) is another game-changer, particularly in supply chain management. IoT devices can provide real-time data on inventory levels, shipment tracking, and equipment performance, enabling businesses to respond proactively to changes. This level of connectivity strengthens both customer and supplier relationships by ensuring reliability and efficiency.

Challenges and Considerations in Implementing Technology

While technology offers immense benefits, implementing CRM and SRM platforms comes with challenges. One of the primary concerns is data quality. Inaccurate or incomplete data can undermine the effectiveness of these tools, leading to flawed insights and decisions. Businesses must invest in robust data governance practices to ensure accuracy and consistency.

Integration can also be complex, especially for organizations using legacy systems. Aligning CRM and SRM tools with existing technologies requires careful planning, technical expertise, and stakeholder collaboration.

User adoption is another critical factor. Even the most advanced platforms can fail to deliver results if employees do not use them effectively. Comprehensive training programs and intuitive interfaces are essential for driving adoption and maximizing ROI.

Data security and privacy are growing concerns in an era of increasing cyber threats. Businesses must ensure that their CRM and SRM systems comply with regulations such as GDPR and maintain robust cybersecurity protocols to protect sensitive information.

The Strategic Impact of Technology in Relationship Management

When implemented effectively, technology transforms relationship management from a reactive process to a proactive, strategic function. CRM tools enable businesses to anticipate customer needs, deliver exceptional experiences, and foster loyalty. SRM platforms empower organizations to build resilient supply chains, drive innovation, and mitigate risks.

The integration of these systems creates a holistic approach to relationship management, aligning customer and supplier strategies with broader organizational goals. As technology continues to evolve, businesses that embrace digital tools and platforms will be better equipped to thrive in an increasingly interconnected and dynamic world.

In conclusion, technology is not just a tool for relationship management—it is the engine that drives it. By leveraging advanced CRM and SRM platforms, businesses can transform relationships into a source of competitive advantage, ensuring long-term success in a rapidly changing environment.

5. Core Principles of Effective Relationship Management: Trust, Communication, and Collaboration

In the dynamic world of business, effective relationship management forms the foundation of sustainable success. Whether dealing with customers or suppliers, the ability to foster strong, reliable, and mutually beneficial relationships is a critical differentiator. While technology and strategy play vital roles, the essence of relationship management lies in core human principles: trust, communication, and collaboration. These principles transcend tools and tactics, serving as the bedrock of meaningful connections and long-term partnerships.

The Pillar of Trust in Relationship Management

Trust is the cornerstone of any successful relationship, whether personal or professional. In business, trust establishes a sense of reliability and confidence between parties. For customers, trust is the assurance that a brand will deliver on its promises. For suppliers, it is the belief that their partnership will be valued and honored.

Building trust requires consistency, transparency, and integrity. Consistency ensures that actions align with words, reinforcing confidence in the organization's reliability. Transparency, on the other hand, involves open and honest communication, even in challenging circumstances. When businesses acknowledge mistakes and work to rectify them, they strengthen their credibility.

Integrity is perhaps the most critical element of trust. Businesses must act ethically and uphold their commitments, even when it is inconvenient. A breach of integrity can irreparably damage relationships, making it one of the most vital components of effective relationship management.

Trust is not a static element—it must be cultivated and nurtured over time. Regular engagement, fulfillment of commitments, and a genuine focus on mutual benefit are key to maintaining and deepening trust in relationships.

The Role of Communication in Building and Sustaining Relationships

Communication is the bridge that connects businesses with their stakeholders. It is through communication that trust is built, expectations are clarified, and challenges are resolved. Effective communication in relationship management is not merely about transmitting information; it is about fostering understanding, alignment, and connection.

In the realm of Customer Relationship Management (CRM), communication involves listening to customer needs, providing timely updates, and delivering personalized experiences. Customers today expect a two-way dialogue with businesses. Listening to their feedback, addressing their concerns, and incorporating their suggestions into products or services create a sense of partnership.

Supplier Relationship Management (SRM) also thrives on effective communication. Regular interaction with suppliers ensures alignment on goals, timelines, and expectations. When businesses communicate openly about their needs and limitations, suppliers can respond proactively, creating a more resilient supply chain.

Communication in relationship management should be clear, concise, and contextually relevant. Overloading stakeholders with information can be as detrimental as providing too little. Tailoring communication to the audience—whether through formal meetings, reports, or digital platforms—ensures that the message is both understood and appreciated.

Non-verbal communication also plays a significant role. Actions often speak louder than words; delivering on promises, adhering to ethical standards, and treating stakeholders with respect convey messages of commitment and value.

Collaboration as a Catalyst for Success

Collaboration is where trust and communication converge to create actionable outcomes. It is the process of working together to achieve shared objectives, leveraging the strengths and insights of all parties involved. Effective collaboration is not merely transactional; it is transformational, creating value that exceeds the sum of individual contributions.

In CRM, collaboration is evident in co-creating value with customers. Whether through loyalty programs, feedback-driven innovation, or community-building initiatives, businesses that collaborate with their customers foster deeper engagement and loyalty. For instance, a company that actively involves its customers in the product design process signals that it values their input, strengthening the relationship.

In SRM, collaboration is critical for achieving supply chain efficiency and innovation. Joint problem-solving, shared risk management, and co-investment in new technologies or processes can enhance the partnership's overall value. Businesses that collaborate effectively with their suppliers are often better equipped to adapt to market changes, mitigate risks, and drive innovation.

Collaboration also extends to internal teams. Cross-functional collaboration ensures that departments such as sales, marketing, procurement, and operations work in harmony to support broader relationship management goals. Silos can hinder relationship effectiveness, making internal alignment a critical aspect of successful collaboration.

The Interplay Between Trust, Communication, and Collaboration

Trust, communication, and collaboration are not isolated principles; they are deeply interconnected. Trust enables open communication, which, in turn, facilitates effective collaboration. For instance, a supplier who trusts a buyer is more likely to share critical information or propose innovative ideas, knowing that their contributions will be valued and respected. Similarly, customers who trust a brand are more likely to provide candid feedback, paving the way for meaningful improvements and collaboration.

Conversely, poor communication can erode trust, while a lack of collaboration can undermine both trust and communication. For example, if a company fails to address customer complaints or neglects supplier feedback, it risks damaging the relationship and its reputation.

Challenges in Upholding These Principles

While the principles of trust, communication, and collaboration are universally acknowledged, implementing them effectively is not without challenges. Misaligned expectations, cultural differences, and competing priorities can hinder relationship management efforts. Additionally, in a digital-first world, the human elements of trust and communication can sometimes be overshadowed by an over-reliance on technology.

Businesses must navigate these challenges by adopting a relationship-centric approach. This involves not only investing in tools and processes but also fostering a culture that values relationships as strategic assets. Leadership commitment, employee training, and continuous improvement are critical for overcoming barriers and ensuring that these principles are upheld.

The Strategic Importance of Core Principles

In today's highly competitive and interconnected world, businesses cannot afford to overlook the importance of trust, communication, and collaboration. These principles are not just about maintaining relationships—they are about creating value, driving innovation, and achieving sustainable growth.

Customers are more likely to remain loyal to brands they trust and feel connected to, while suppliers are more likely to prioritize businesses that value collaboration. By embedding these principles into their relationship management strategies, organizations can build resilient networks, enhance stakeholder satisfaction, and secure a competitive edge.

In conclusion, trust, communication, and collaboration are the lifeblood of effective relationship management. They are the principles that transform transactions into partnerships, challenges into opportunities, and interactions into meaningful connections. By prioritizing these principles, businesses can not only navigate the complexities of modern relationship management but also thrive in a landscape defined by constant change and increasing expectations.

Part 2: Building a Customer-Centric CRM System

6. Understanding Customer Needs: Insights Through Data and Feedback

In the modern marketplace, understanding customer needs is no longer a luxury—it is a necessity. As customer expectations continue to rise, businesses must focus on gaining deep insights into what their customers truly want. This understanding is the foundation of a customer-centric approach and the key to developing a CRM system that drives engagement, loyalty, and long-term success.

The art and science of understanding customer needs hinge on two critical components: the ability to collect and analyze relevant data and the commitment to actively listen to customer feedback. Together, these elements provide a comprehensive picture of customer preferences, behaviors, and pain points, empowering organizations to design personalized experiences and value-driven solutions.

The Strategic Importance of Understanding Customer Needs

Understanding customer needs is central to creating value and maintaining competitive advantage. In a crowded market, products and services are often similar, and the differentiating factor becomes the customer experience. Businesses that anticipate and fulfill customer needs not only retain existing customers but also attract new ones through positive word-of-mouth and reputation.

Moreover, aligning offerings with customer needs minimizes the risk of wasted resources. When businesses have a clear understanding of their customers, they can focus their efforts on what truly matters, avoiding unnecessary features or misaligned marketing campaigns.

Customer needs also evolve over time. Regularly revisiting and updating insights ensures that businesses remain relevant and adaptable in a dynamic environment.

The Role of Data in Understanding Customer Needs

Data is the backbone of modern CRM systems, providing the raw material for actionable insights. From purchase history and website interactions to demographic information and social media activity, every data point offers a glimpse into the customer's world.

CRM platforms are designed to centralize and organize this data, creating a unified view of the customer. By aggregating information from multiple touchpoints, businesses can identify patterns and trends that reveal customer preferences and behaviors. For example, data analysis might show that a particular segment prefers online shopping during specific hours, enabling targeted marketing efforts.

Predictive analytics takes this a step further by using historical data to forecast future behavior. For instance, a retail CRM system might predict which customers are likely to make repeat purchases during the holiday season, allowing businesses to design tailored promotions.

Data visualization tools within CRM platforms, such as dashboards and heat maps, make it easier to interpret complex data sets. These tools highlight key metrics and trends, ensuring that insights are accessible to decision-makers across the organization.

The Power of Customer Feedback

While data provides quantitative insights, customer feedback offers the qualitative perspective needed to understand emotions, expectations, and experiences. Feedback channels, such as surveys, reviews, focus groups, and direct conversations, are invaluable for capturing the voice of the customer (VoC).

Customer surveys remain one of the most effective tools for gathering feedback. Structured surveys with targeted questions can reveal satisfaction levels, identify pain points, and highlight areas for improvement. Open-ended questions, in particular, allow customers to share detailed insights in their own words, providing a richer understanding of their needs.

Social media platforms have also become a goldmine for customer feedback. By monitoring mentions, comments, and reviews, businesses can gauge sentiment and identify emerging trends. Social listening tools, integrated into many CRM systems, help track brand reputation and customer perception in real-time.

Proactively seeking feedback demonstrates that a business values its customers' opinions. When customers feel heard, they are more likely to engage with the brand and provide constructive input.

Balancing Data and Feedback

While data and feedback are both essential, they serve different purposes and must be balanced for a holistic understanding of customer needs. Data provides the "what"—identifying behaviors and trends—while feedback reveals the "why" behind those patterns. For example, data might show a decline in sales for a particular product, but feedback can uncover the reason, such as quality issues or unmet expectations.

Integrating data and feedback within a CRM system ensures that insights are comprehensive and actionable. Advanced CRM platforms offer features that combine these elements, such as sentiment analysis tools that interpret feedback in the context of customer behavior.

Challenges in Understanding Customer Needs

Despite its importance, understanding customer needs is not without challenges. One common obstacle is data overload. With the proliferation of digital channels, businesses often collect vast amounts of data, much of which is unstructured or irrelevant. Without proper tools and strategies for filtering and analyzing this data, it can be difficult to extract meaningful insights.

Another challenge is the accuracy and reliability of data. Outdated or incomplete information can lead to flawed conclusions and misguided decisions. Regular data cleansing and validation processes are essential for maintaining data quality.

Feedback collection also presents challenges. Customers may be reluctant to provide feedback due to survey fatigue or a lack of perceived benefit. To overcome this, businesses should design engaging feedback mechanisms and communicate how the input will be used to improve their offerings.

Privacy concerns are another critical consideration. Customers are increasingly aware of how their data is collected and used. Transparency and compliance with data protection regulations, such as GDPR, are vital for maintaining trust and securing consent.

Best Practices for Understanding Customer Needs

To effectively understand customer needs, businesses should adopt a structured approach:

1. **Segment the Customer Base**
   Dividing customers into segments based on demographics, behavior, or preferences allows businesses to tailor insights and strategies to specific groups.

2. **Leverage Advanced Analytics**
   Investing in predictive and prescriptive analytics enhances the ability to forecast and address customer needs proactively.

3. **Foster a Feedback-Driven Culture**
   Encouraging customer-facing teams to actively seek and share feedback ensures that insights are integrated across the organization.

4. **Invest in Training and Tools**
   Equipping employees with the skills and technology needed to interpret data and feedback improves the quality of insights and decision-making.

5. **Continuously Monitor and Adapt**
   Customer needs are dynamic. Regularly updating insights ensures that businesses stay ahead of evolving expectations.

The Strategic Impact of Understanding Customer Needs

When businesses truly understand their customers, they can create experiences that resonate on a personal level. This not only drives customer satisfaction and loyalty but also enhances profitability. Satisfied customers are more likely to make repeat purchases, recommend the brand to others, and engage with new offerings.

Furthermore, a deep understanding of customer needs enables innovation. By identifying unmet needs and emerging trends, businesses can develop products and services that anticipate and address future demands.

In conclusion, understanding customer needs is the heart of a customer-centric CRM system. By combining the power of data and feedback, businesses can unlock insights that drive meaningful connections, informed decisions, and sustainable growth.

Understanding Customer Needs: Insights Through Data and Feedback

In the modern marketplace, understanding customer needs is no longer a luxury—it is a necessity. As customer expectations continue to rise, businesses must focus on gaining deep insights into what their customers truly want. This understanding is the foundation of a customer-centric approach and the key to developing a CRM system that drives engagement, loyalty, and long-term success.

The art and science of understanding customer needs hinge on two critical components: the ability to collect and analyze relevant data and the commitment to actively listen to customer feedback. Together, these elements provide a comprehensive picture of customer preferences, behaviors, and pain points, empowering organizations to design personalized experiences and value-driven solutions.

The Strategic Importance of Understanding Customer Needs

Understanding customer needs is central to creating value and maintaining competitive advantage. In a crowded market, products and services are often similar, and the differentiating factor becomes the customer experience. Businesses that anticipate and fulfill customer needs not only retain existing customers but also attract new ones through positive word-of-mouth and reputation.

Moreover, aligning offerings with customer needs minimizes the risk of wasted resources. When businesses have a clear understanding of their customers, they can focus their efforts on what truly matters, avoiding unnecessary features or misaligned marketing campaigns.

Customer needs also evolve over time. Regularly revisiting and updating insights ensures that businesses remain relevant and adaptable in a dynamic environment.

The Role of Data in Understanding Customer Needs

Data is the backbone of modern CRM systems, providing the raw material for actionable insights. From purchase history and website interactions to demographic information and social media activity, every data point offers a glimpse into the customer's world.

CRM platforms are designed to centralize and organize this data, creating a unified view of the customer. By aggregating information from multiple touchpoints, businesses can identify patterns and trends that reveal customer preferences and behaviors. For example, data analysis might show that a particular segment prefers online shopping during specific hours, enabling targeted marketing efforts.

Predictive analytics takes this a step further by using historical data to forecast future behavior. For instance, a retail CRM system might predict which customers are likely to make repeat purchases during the holiday season, allowing businesses to design tailored promotions.

Data visualization tools within CRM platforms, such as dashboards and heat maps, make it easier to interpret complex data sets. These tools highlight key metrics and trends, ensuring that insights are accessible to decision-makers across the organization.

The Power of Customer Feedback

While data provides quantitative insights, customer feedback offers the qualitative perspective needed to understand emotions, expectations, and experiences. Feedback channels, such as surveys, reviews, focus groups, and direct conversations, are invaluable for capturing the voice of the customer (VoC).

Customer surveys remain one of the most effective tools for gathering feedback. Structured surveys with targeted questions can reveal satisfaction levels, identify pain points, and highlight areas for improvement. Open-ended questions, in particular, allow customers to share detailed insights in their own words, providing a richer understanding of their needs.

Social media platforms have also become a goldmine for customer feedback. By monitoring mentions, comments, and reviews, businesses can gauge sentiment and identify emerging trends. Social listening tools, integrated into many CRM systems, help track brand reputation and customer perception in real-time.

Proactively seeking feedback demonstrates that a business values its customers' opinions. When customers feel heard, they are more likely to engage with the brand and provide constructive input.

Balancing Data and Feedback

While data and feedback are both essential, they serve different purposes and must be balanced for a holistic understanding of customer needs. Data provides the "what"—identifying behaviors and trends—while feedback reveals the "why" behind those patterns. For example, data might show a decline in sales for a particular product, but feedback can uncover the reason, such as quality issues or unmet expectations.

Integrating data and feedback within a CRM system ensures that insights are comprehensive and actionable. Advanced CRM platforms offer features that combine these elements, such as sentiment analysis tools that interpret feedback in the context of customer behavior.

Challenges in Understanding Customer Needs

Despite its importance, understanding customer needs is not without challenges. One common obstacle is data overload. With the proliferation of digital channels, businesses often collect vast amounts of data, much of which is unstructured or irrelevant. Without proper tools and strategies for filtering and analyzing this data, it can be difficult to extract meaningful insights.

Another challenge is the accuracy and reliability of data. Outdated or incomplete information can lead to flawed conclusions and misguided decisions. Regular data cleansing and validation processes are essential for maintaining data quality.

Feedback collection also presents challenges. Customers may be reluctant to provide feedback due to survey fatigue or a lack of perceived benefit. To overcome this, businesses should design engaging feedback mechanisms and communicate how the input will be used to improve their offerings.

Privacy concerns are another critical consideration. Customers are increasingly aware of how their data is collected and used. Transparency and compliance with data protection regulations, such as GDPR, are vital for maintaining trust and securing consent.

Best Practices for Understanding Customer Needs

To effectively understand customer needs, businesses should adopt a structured approach:

Segment the Customer Base
Dividing customers into segments based on demographics, behavior, or preferences allows businesses to tailor insights and strategies to specific groups.

Leverage Advanced Analytics
Investing in predictive and prescriptive analytics enhances the ability to forecast and address customer needs proactively.

Foster a Feedback-Driven Culture
Encouraging customer-facing teams to actively seek and share feedback ensures that insights are integrated across the organization.

Invest in Training and Tools
Equipping employees with the skills and technology needed to interpret data and feedback improves the quality of insights and decision-making.

Continuously Monitor and Adapt
Customer needs are dynamic. Regularly updating insights ensures that businesses stay ahead of evolving expectations.

The Strategic Impact of Understanding Customer Needs

When businesses truly understand their customers, they can create experiences that resonate on a personal level. This not only drives customer satisfaction and loyalty but also enhances profitability. Satisfied customers are more likely to make repeat purchases, recommend the brand to others, and engage with new offerings.

Furthermore, a deep understanding of customer needs enables innovation. By identifying unmet needs and emerging trends, businesses can develop products and services that anticipate and address future demands.

In conclusion, understanding customer needs is the heart of a customer-centric CRM system. By combining the power of data and feedback, businesses can unlock insights that drive meaningful connections, informed decisions, and sustainable growth.

CRM Tools and Platforms: Choosing the Right Solution for Your Business

In the digital age, a robust Customer Relationship Management (CRM) system is a pivotal asset for businesses seeking to maintain competitive advantages. A CRM system not only helps in managing and analyzing customer interactions and data but also plays a central role in streamlining operations, enhancing customer experience, and driving business growth. However, with a multitude of CRM tools and platforms available, businesses often face the challenge of selecting the one best suited to their needs, scale, and objectives.

Choosing the right CRM solution is a critical decision that requires careful consideration of various factors. It involves understanding the specific needs of your business, evaluating the capabilities of different CRM tools, and determining how they integrate with existing processes. The right CRM can transform how your business interacts with customers, but selecting the wrong one can result in wasted resources and missed opportunities.

The Importance of CRM Systems in Business Operations

CRM systems are essential for businesses of all sizes, whether they are startups looking to build relationships or established enterprises aiming to streamline customer interaction. At its core, a CRM system centralizes customer data—such as contact details, communication history, transaction records, and behavioral patterns—into a single platform, making it easier for businesses to access and analyze the information.

A well-chosen CRM system enables businesses to understand customer needs better, personalize their services, track sales leads, automate marketing efforts, and manage customer service more effectively. By centralizing data, CRMs ensure that every customer touchpoint is informed, reducing inefficiencies and errors.

Additionally, CRM systems offer valuable analytics that help businesses measure performance, identify trends, and make data-driven decisions. This insight allows for more targeted and effective strategies in customer engagement, marketing, sales, and service, resulting in improved customer satisfaction and loyalty.

Evaluating CRM Solutions: Key Considerations

When selecting the right CRM tool for your business, there are several key factors to consider:

1. Business Needs and Objectives

Every business has unique requirements, and the CRM system must align with these needs. Whether your focus is on sales, customer service, or marketing, there are CRMs designed specifically for each area. For instance, a business with an extensive customer service department may prioritize a CRM system with powerful support and ticket management features. In contrast, a sales-driven organization may need a CRM that specializes in lead management and sales forecasting.

Understanding your business's core objectives will help narrow down your options. If customer support is your main focus, ensure the CRM can handle multi-channel communication, automated ticketing, and knowledge management. If your focus is lead generation, look for CRMs with strong analytics, customer segmentation, and lead nurturing features.

2. User-Friendliness

A CRM system's usability plays a pivotal role in its adoption and success within the organization. The complexity of a system can determine how effectively employees engage with the tool, so ease of use is a significant factor when evaluating CRM platforms.

Look for a CRM that is intuitive and easy to navigate. The last thing you want is a system that requires extensive training and constant troubleshooting. A user-friendly interface will ensure that your team members can quickly adopt the system, resulting in faster implementation and greater user satisfaction.

3. Customization and Flexibility

Every business operates differently, and your CRM should be flexible enough to adapt to those unique needs. A CRM that offers customization options allows you to tailor the platform to your workflow, data requirements, and business processes.

Customization can range from simple features like branding and field modification to more complex workflows and integrations. Some CRM systems allow for advanced customization, such as custom reporting, automated actions, and tailored sales pipelines. This flexibility ensures that the CRM aligns perfectly with the business model, rather than forcing the business to adjust to the tool.

4. Integration with Existing Tools

In most cases, businesses already rely on various software tools for accounting, marketing, project management, and communication. For a CRM to be effective, it must seamlessly integrate with these tools to centralize data and optimize workflows.

Look for CRM solutions that integrate with tools such as email marketing platforms, social media management systems, and ERP solutions. This eliminates the need for duplicate data entry, reduces human errors, and ensures that all departments are working from the same data set. Integrations with popular platforms like Microsoft Office, Google Workspace, and Slack can enhance your CRM's utility and improve team collaboration.

5. Scalability

As your business grows, so too will your CRM needs. It is essential to choose a CRM system that can scale with your business. Whether you anticipate expanding to new markets, increasing your customer base, or adding new functionalities, the CRM should accommodate future growth without requiring a complete overhaul.

Scalability means that the CRM can handle increasing volumes of data, users, and complex workflows. Many modern CRM solutions offer modular functionality, allowing businesses to add features as needed, such as marketing automation, analytics, or artificial intelligence tools, as their requirements evolve.

6. Cloud vs. On-Premise CRM

CRM solutions come in two primary deployment models: cloud-based and on-premise. Both options have their advantages and disadvantages, and the right choice will depend on your business's preferences and resources.

Cloud-based CRMs are hosted remotely and accessed through the internet. These platforms are typically more affordable to implement, as they do not require expensive hardware or IT infrastructure. They also offer the flexibility of remote access, making them ideal for businesses with distributed teams or mobile workforces. However, businesses must ensure they have reliable internet connections and trust the vendor's data security measures.

On-premise CRMs, on the other hand, are installed and maintained on the company's own servers. This option provides greater control over the system, as well as increased security, especially for businesses that handle sensitive customer information. However, on-premise systems come with higher upfront costs and may require dedicated IT resources for maintenance and updates.

7. Cost and ROI

The cost of CRM tools can vary significantly depending on the features, deployment model, and user count. Businesses must weigh the cost against the potential return on investment (ROI) the CRM system can deliver. Consider factors such as improved customer retention, increased sales, better data insights, and enhanced team efficiency when calculating the ROI.

Many CRM platforms offer tiered pricing models, allowing businesses to start with basic features and upgrade as needed. Additionally, subscription-based cloud CRMs often offer lower initial costs and predictable ongoing expenses, making them easier to budget for.

Popular CRM Tools and Platforms

There is no one-size-fits-all CRM solution, and the market is filled with a variety of options that cater to different business needs and sizes. Some of the most popular CRM tools include:

- **Salesforce**: Known for its powerful and highly customizable features, Salesforce is a leader in the CRM market. It is particularly well-suited for large enterprises with complex needs, offering comprehensive solutions for sales, marketing, customer service, and analytics.

- **HubSpot CRM**: HubSpot is a cloud-based CRM that is favored by small to mid-sized businesses for its ease of use and comprehensive set of features. It includes tools for lead management, email marketing, and customer segmentation, with a focus on inbound marketing.

- **Zoho CRM**: Zoho CRM is an affordable and scalable option for businesses of all sizes. It offers a wide range of features, including sales automation, customer analytics, and integration with third-party tools, making it an ideal choice for growing businesses.

- **Microsoft Dynamics 365**: This platform is perfect for organizations that rely heavily on Microsoft products. It integrates seamlessly with Office 365 and provides advanced analytics, workflow automation, and AI-powered insights.

- **Pipedrive**: Known for its simple user interface and sales pipeline management features, Pipedrive is best suited for small to mid-sized businesses looking for a straightforward CRM solution that helps streamline their sales process.

Selecting the right CRM tool is a critical decision that can significantly impact your business's ability to build and maintain strong customer relationships. By evaluating factors such as business needs, ease of use, customization options, integration capabilities, scalability, and cost, businesses can identify a CRM solution that aligns with their goals and supports long-term growth. With the right CRM in place, businesses can not only manage customer relationships more effectively but also unlock new opportunities for innovation, customer satisfaction, and success.

8. Personalization in CRM: Leveraging Data for Tailored Experiences

In today's competitive marketplace, customer experience has become a critical factor in business success. Customers now expect businesses to understand their preferences, anticipate their needs, and deliver personalized experiences across all touchpoints. In response to this demand, companies are increasingly turning to Customer Relationship Management (CRM) systems to help them achieve a higher level of personalization. By leveraging data effectively, businesses can create tailored experiences that not only improve customer satisfaction but also drive loyalty and increase revenue.

Personalization in CRM goes beyond just addressing customers by their names in an email. It encompasses a comprehensive approach that uses customer data to deliver individualized experiences based on preferences, behaviors, past interactions, and anticipated needs. By leveraging advanced CRM tools and platforms, businesses can gain valuable insights into their customer base, create personalized marketing messages, optimize sales efforts, and improve customer service.

The Power of Personalization in Customer Relationships

Personalization has proven to be one of the most effective strategies for building and nurturing long-term customer relationships. When done right, personalized experiences foster a deeper emotional connection between the customer and the brand. This connection can lead to greater customer loyalty, higher retention rates, and increased lifetime value.

Personalization in CRM allows businesses to provide customers with a sense of exclusivity, where they feel like they are being recognized and valued. This personalized approach not only makes customers more likely to engage with the business but also strengthens brand affinity. Whether it's personalized email marketing, product recommendations, or customer service interactions, personalization is about making every experience more relevant and meaningful to the customer.

In fact, studies have shown that customers are more likely to make a purchase from brands that provide personalized experiences. According to research by Epsilon, 80% of consumers are more likely to purchase from a brand that offers a personalized experience. This highlights the growing importance of personalization in achieving a competitive edge in today's crowded market.

Understanding Customer Data: The Key to Personalization

To effectively personalize customer interactions, businesses must first gather and analyze customer data. Customer data comes in many forms, including demographic information, purchase history, browsing behavior, engagement with marketing campaigns, and customer feedback. Each of these data points can provide valuable insights into a customer's preferences, needs, and behaviors.

A CRM system serves as the central hub for collecting and storing this data. By consolidating all customer information in one place, businesses can create a comprehensive customer profile that provides a 360-degree view of the individual customer. This allows businesses to better understand their customers' behavior and anticipate their needs.

For example, an e-commerce business can track customers' browsing history and purchase patterns to suggest relevant products. By analyzing data such as the frequency of visits, time spent on specific pages, and abandoned cart items, the CRM can suggest targeted offers and content that are more likely to result in a sale. Similarly, businesses can use demographic information such as location, age, and gender to personalize email marketing campaigns, tailoring content to each segment of their audience.

However, collecting customer data is not enough. Businesses must also have the right tools to analyze and derive actionable insights from the data. Modern CRM systems offer advanced analytics capabilities, such as segmentation, predictive modeling, and customer lifetime value forecasting. These tools allow businesses to gain a deeper understanding of their customers and create more effective personalization strategies.

Segmentation: The Foundation of Personalization

One of the first steps in personalizing customer experiences is segmenting your customer base. Segmentation involves dividing your customers into groups based on shared characteristics, behaviors, or needs. By segmenting your customers, you can tailor your messaging and offers to be more relevant to each group, rather than using a one-size-fits-all approach.

Segmentation can be based on a variety of factors, including demographics (age, gender, income), psychographics (values, interests, lifestyle), purchase behavior (frequency, recency, spend), and engagement level (active vs. inactive customers). A CRM system can automate this segmentation process by categorizing customers based on these criteria and updating the segments as new data comes in.

For example, a retail business might segment customers into groups such as high-value shoppers, occasional buyers, and first-time visitors. Each group can then receive tailored marketing messages that resonate with their specific behavior and needs. High-value shoppers might receive exclusive offers or loyalty rewards, while first-time visitors may receive a welcome email with a special discount for their next purchase.

Segmentation is a powerful tool for delivering personalized experiences at scale. Instead of manually tailoring every interaction, businesses can automate the process by creating personalized workflows based on customer segments. This not only saves time and resources but also ensures that each customer receives the most relevant content and offers.

Personalized Marketing: Creating Relevant and Engaging Campaigns

Personalized marketing is a cornerstone of CRM personalization. With access to customer data and segmentation tools, businesses can craft highly targeted marketing campaigns that speak directly to the individual's interests and preferences. This can be achieved through various channels, such as email, social media, SMS, and website content.

Email marketing, in particular, benefits significantly from personalization. Rather than sending generic newsletters to a broad audience, businesses can create dynamic email content that changes based on the recipient's behavior. For instance, an online retailer can send personalized product recommendations based on a customer's past purchases or browsing activity. Alternatively, a SaaS company might offer a special discount or upgrade opportunity for customers who have shown interest in a specific feature but have not yet purchased.

Personalized email campaigns can also be used to nurture leads and improve conversion rates. A well-timed follow-up email with personalized content can be the difference between a potential customer abandoning their cart or completing a purchase.

Social media is another effective channel for personalization. By leveraging customer data from CRM systems, businesses can tailor their social media posts, ads, and promotions to the individual. This can be done by targeting specific customer segments with tailored offers or personalized messages that resonate with their interests and behaviors.

Personalized Customer Service: Anticipating Customer Needs

Personalization in CRM goes beyond marketing. It also plays a significant role in improving customer service interactions. Customers want to feel heard and valued when they reach out for support. By using CRM data, businesses can deliver a more personalized and efficient customer service experience.

When a customer contacts a business, customer service representatives can access their complete history with the brand, including past purchases, service requests, and interactions. This provides valuable context for the representative, allowing them to offer solutions faster and more effectively. For example, if a customer is experiencing an issue with a product they purchased, the representative can immediately see if the customer has already requested a refund or exchanged the item in the past. This enables the representative to address the issue in a more personalized and informed manner.

In addition, businesses can use predictive analytics to anticipate customer needs before they even arise. By analyzing past interactions and behavior patterns, businesses can predict when a customer might need assistance or may be at risk of churning. This allows businesses to take proactive steps to engage with the customer and prevent issues from escalating.

Furthermore, personalized customer service can be enhanced by using omnichannel support. A CRM system can centralize customer service data across multiple touchpoints, such as phone, email, live chat, and social media, providing a seamless and consistent experience for the customer. This ensures that customers do not have to repeat themselves or re-explain their issues when switching between channels.

The Challenges of Personalization in CRM

While personalization offers immense benefits, it also comes with its challenges. One of the biggest hurdles is data privacy. With increasing concerns over data security and privacy regulations such as GDPR, businesses must ensure that they are handling customer data responsibly and ethically. Customers need to trust that their personal information is being used appropriately and securely, or they may abandon the brand altogether.

Another challenge is ensuring the accuracy and quality of customer data. CRM systems are only as effective as the data they rely on, and inaccurate or outdated information can lead to poor personalization efforts. Regular data cleansing and validation are essential to maintain the integrity of customer profiles and ensure that personalized experiences are based on reliable information.

Lastly, personalization at scale can be difficult for businesses with large customer bases. Creating tailored experiences for thousands or millions of customers requires advanced CRM systems, automation, and artificial intelligence to manage effectively. Without the right tools and strategies in place, businesses may struggle to deliver meaningful personalization at scale.

Conclusion

Personalization in CRM is more than just a trend—it is a necessity for businesses seeking to stay relevant and competitive in a customer-driven marketplace. By leveraging data and insights, businesses can create tailored experiences that resonate with customers, improve engagement, and foster loyalty. From personalized marketing campaigns to customer service interactions, CRM systems enable businesses to deliver a more individualized approach that enhances the overall customer experience. However, successful personalization requires the right technology, data management practices, and a commitment to data privacy. When executed correctly, personalization can transform the customer relationship and drive long-term business success.

9. Automation in CRM: Streamlining Processes with Technology

Automation in CRM: Streamlining Processes with Technology

In the modern business environment, where customer expectations are constantly rising, companies are under increasing pressure to deliver seamless, personalized, and timely interactions at scale. Customer Relationship Management (CRM) systems, which serve as the backbone of many business operations, offer the solution to this challenge by integrating technology to automate key processes. CRM automation helps streamline various tasks, improving efficiency, enhancing customer experience, and freeing up valuable human resources for more strategic work. By leveraging automation in CRM, businesses can optimize their workflows, enhance data accuracy, reduce operational costs, and create more meaningful, real-time engagement with customers.

CRM automation isn't just about replacing human effort with machines; it's about using technology to improve the quality, consistency, and timeliness of interactions with customers, suppliers, and prospects. The ability to automate routine tasks allows organizations to focus on higher-value activities, such as nurturing relationships, analyzing data for insights, and making strategic decisions that drive growth. This chapter will explore the various ways in which automation in CRM can streamline processes and enhance business outcomes.

The Role of CRM Automation in Modern Business

Automation in CRM has become essential for businesses to stay competitive. As companies grow and their customer base expands, manually handling customer interactions and data management becomes increasingly impractical. Traditional methods of managing customer relationships through spreadsheets, phone calls, and emails are no longer efficient or effective for businesses that need to scale. CRM automation addresses this problem by automating repetitive tasks, integrating processes, and ensuring that data flows seamlessly between different functions within an organization.

At its core, CRM automation is designed to make interactions more efficient and to provide consistent, timely, and personalized experiences to customers. This can include anything from automatically scheduling follow-up emails, sending targeted offers to customers based on their behavior, or automatically assigning leads to the appropriate sales representatives. The goal is not only to make day-to-day operations easier but also to create a more organized, proactive approach to managing customer relationships.

Types of CRM Automation

CRM systems offer a wide range of automation features that can benefit businesses in various ways. The following are some of the key types of automation that organizations can use to streamline processes:

Lead Management Automation

One of the most common applications of CRM automation is in lead management. Lead capture, qualification, and nurturing can be automated to ensure that potential customers receive timely attention without manual intervention. For example, when a customer fills out a contact form on a website, the CRM can automatically capture that lead, assign it to the appropriate sales team member, and send an initial follow-up email. Additionally, lead nurturing campaigns can be set up to automatically send personalized content, reminders, or promotions to leads based on their stage in the sales funnel. This ensures that no leads are neglected, and sales representatives can focus on closing deals rather than chasing after leads.

Email Marketing Automation

One of the most powerful forms of CRM automation is email marketing. Businesses can set up automated email campaigns that send personalized messages to customers or leads based on specific triggers or timelines. For example, a customer who abandons their cart on an e-commerce website can automatically receive a reminder email with a special offer to complete their purchase. Similarly, businesses can send birthday emails, thank-you notes, or product recommendations based on past purchase behavior. Automated emails ensure that customers receive timely and relevant content, helping to build stronger relationships and increase conversion rates.

Customer Service Automation

CRM automation can also play a vital role in enhancing customer service operations. With the help of automation, businesses can provide 24/7 support to their customers, improve response times, and resolve issues more efficiently. Chatbots, for example, are widely used in CRM systems to handle basic customer inquiries and direct them to the appropriate resources. These bots can answer frequently asked questions, provide product recommendations, or escalate issues to human agents when necessary. Additionally, CRM automation can be used to automatically assign customer service tickets to the appropriate team members based on the issue type, ensuring that inquiries are resolved quickly and by the right person.

Task and Workflow Automation

CRM systems can also automate routine tasks and workflows that are often time-consuming. For instance, a sales representative might need to follow up with a lead after a meeting, log interaction notes, update the CRM database with new information, or schedule the next step in the sales process. With CRM automation, many of these tasks can be done automatically. After a meeting, for example, the CRM can automatically send a follow-up email to the lead with relevant information, schedule a reminder for the next call, and update the customer's record with the latest details. This helps to maintain consistency in the sales process and ensures that no important tasks are overlooked.

Data Management and Reporting Automation

A major aspect of CRM automation is the ability to collect, organize, and analyze data automatically. Manually entering and updating customer information can be time-consuming and prone to errors.

Automation streamlines this process by automatically updating customer profiles with relevant data from emails, phone calls, or interactions on social media. This data is then used to generate reports that provide valuable insights into customer behavior, sales performance, and other key metrics. Automated reporting can save businesses significant time and effort, allowing decision-makers to focus on analyzing the results and making informed decisions.

Sales Pipeline Automation

CRM automation can also be highly effective in managing the sales pipeline. A well-defined sales process often involves several stages, such as lead qualification, prospecting, presenting, and closing. Automating these stages ensures that sales representatives follow the right steps at the right time and that no opportunities are missed. For example, as a lead moves through the pipeline, the CRM can automatically update the stage, notify the appropriate sales rep, and send follow-up emails or reminders. This helps sales teams stay on top of their tasks, improves accountability, and ensures a more organized and efficient sales process.

Integration with Other Business Systems

CRM systems often integrate with other business systems, such as marketing automation, accounting, and inventory management software. By integrating CRM with these platforms, businesses can automate data flow between different departments, reducing the need for manual input and minimizing the risk of errors. For example, when a customer places an order, the CRM system can automatically update the inventory management system, trigger a confirmation email to the customer, and notify the sales team. This integration streamlines operations across the business and ensures that all departments have access to the same accurate, up-to-date customer information.

Benefits of CRM Automation

The use of automation in CRM systems brings numerous benefits to businesses, many of which directly impact customer satisfaction and organizational efficiency. The key benefits include:

Increased Efficiency

Automation allows businesses to complete routine tasks faster and more accurately, which leads to significant improvements in overall efficiency. Tasks that would otherwise take hours or days, such as data entry, follow-up emails, and report generation, can be completed in a matter of seconds with CRM automation. This frees up time for employees to focus on higher-value activities that require human judgment and creativity.

Enhanced Customer Experience

Automation enables businesses to provide a more consistent and timely experience for customers. For example, automated emails ensure that customers receive relevant information at the right time, while chatbots provide instant responses to common questions. This enhances the customer experience by delivering personalized, real-time interactions and improving satisfaction levels.

Improved Lead Management

With CRM automation, businesses can capture, track, and nurture leads more effectively. By automatically assigning leads to the right team members, tracking interactions, and sending personalized content, companies can improve conversion rates and close deals faster.

Cost Savings

Automation can also help businesses reduce operational costs by eliminating the need for manual labor in repetitive tasks. CRM automation reduces the chance of human error, increases the speed at which tasks are completed, and minimizes the need for extensive training or additional hires.

Better Data Accuracy and Insights

Automating data management ensures that customer information is always up-to-date and accurate. This leads to better decision-making, as businesses can rely on accurate data when planning marketing strategies, sales efforts, and customer service initiatives. Automated reporting also provides valuable insights into customer behavior and business performance, enabling companies to make data-driven decisions.

Challenges of CRM Automation

While CRM automation offers numerous advantages, it is not without its challenges. One of the main obstacles is the potential for over-automation, where businesses may automate too many processes at the expense of human touch. While automation can improve efficiency, some customer interactions still require a personal connection. Striking the right balance between automation and human interaction is critical to ensure that customers feel valued and understood.

Another challenge is the complexity of integrating CRM automation with existing systems. For businesses with legacy software or disjointed platforms, integrating CRM with other systems can be a time-consuming and costly process. Additionally, businesses must ensure that employees are adequately trained to use the new automated tools effectively.

Data privacy and security are also major concerns when automating CRM processes. Businesses must ensure that customer data is handled securely and that automation systems comply with relevant privacy regulations. Failing to protect sensitive data can lead to loss of trust, legal ramifications, and reputational damage.

Conclusion

Automation in CRM is a powerful tool that can help businesses streamline their processes, enhance customer interactions, and improve operational efficiency. By automating tasks such as lead management, email marketing, customer service, and reporting, businesses can reduce manual labor, improve data accuracy, and create a more personalized customer experience. However, it is important to carefully consider the balance between automation and human interaction to ensure that customers still feel valued and understood. When implemented correctly, CRM automation can significantly improve business outcomes, allowing organizations to scale more efficiently and effectively engage with their customers.

10. Measuring CRM Success: Key Performance Indicators (KPIs) and Metrics

In today's competitive business environment, companies have adopted Customer Relationship Management (CRM) systems to better understand, interact with, and serve their customers. However, the success of these CRM initiatives cannot simply be assumed. It is essential to measure the effectiveness of CRM systems and their impact on the organization's overall performance. Measuring CRM success is not just about tracking the volume of customer interactions or the number of sales made; it involves a more comprehensive assessment of the system's ability to achieve strategic business objectives, enhance customer experiences, and drive growth. To accurately assess this success, businesses must rely on key performance indicators (KPIs) and metrics that align with their specific goals, customer relationship strategies, and operational efficiency targets.

This chapter delves into the most important KPIs and metrics used to measure CRM success, discussing how to identify, track, and interpret them to gain valuable insights into CRM performance. Furthermore, it provides a detailed understanding of the role of data-driven decision-making in CRM and highlights how businesses can leverage these metrics to fine-tune their customer relationship management strategies.

The Importance of Measuring CRM Success

Measuring CRM success is essential for ensuring that the investment in CRM technology and strategies delivers tangible results. Many businesses implement CRM systems to improve customer satisfaction, increase retention, boost sales, and enhance overall efficiency. Without defining specific success metrics, however, organizations may struggle to determine whether their CRM initiatives are delivering on these objectives. Metrics allow businesses to quantify the outcomes of CRM efforts and provide clear data that can be used for further decision-making, optimization, and resource allocation.

By establishing the right KPIs and measuring them consistently, companies gain insights into customer behavior, sales performance, service quality, and the effectiveness of marketing campaigns. These insights are crucial for refining CRM strategies, improving customer interactions, and ultimately achieving long-term business success. Furthermore, the measurement of CRM performance empowers organizations to demonstrate the value of CRM systems to stakeholders, whether it be upper management, investors, or partners.

Defining Key Performance Indicators (KPIs) for CRM

KPIs are measurable values that demonstrate how effectively a company is achieving its key business objectives. In the context of CRM, KPIs help evaluate how well a CRM system is managing customer relationships and contributing to the organization's goals. The right KPIs are those that provide actionable insights, align with business objectives, and offer a clear picture of how CRM initiatives are performing. These indicators go beyond traditional metrics such as sales figures and delve into the quality of customer relationships, engagement levels, and the efficiency of CRM processes.

Some KPIs are specifically tied to sales and marketing, while others focus on customer service or operational efficiency. The choice of KPIs will depend on the business's goals, whether those are focused on increasing revenue, enhancing customer retention, improving customer service response times, or streamlining internal processes.

Sales and Revenue-Related KPIs

The direct link between CRM systems and sales is one of the primary areas of focus when measuring CRM success. A CRM system is designed to support the sales team by tracking leads, managing opportunities, and improving conversion rates. As a result, several sales-related KPIs are essential for evaluating CRM performance.

Sales Growth
Sales growth is one of the most straightforward and significant KPIs for CRM success. It measures the increase in sales over a specific

period, such as monthly, quarterly, or yearly. CRM systems contribute to sales growth by streamlining sales processes, improving lead conversion, and enabling more personalized customer interactions. By tracking sales growth, businesses can assess the direct impact of CRM tools and strategies on revenue generation.

Lead Conversion Rate

The lead conversion rate measures the percentage of leads that are successfully converted into paying customers. A CRM system allows sales teams to nurture leads more effectively through automated follow-ups, tailored messaging, and a structured sales pipeline. By analyzing lead conversion rates, businesses can gauge how well their CRM system is facilitating the movement of prospects through the sales funnel and whether the sales team is effectively closing deals.

Average Deal Size

CRM systems allow businesses to track not only the number of deals but also the value of each deal. By measuring the average deal size, businesses can understand how well they are leveraging CRM to upsell or cross-sell products and services to customers. An increase in average deal size suggests that CRM strategies, such as personalized product recommendations or targeted offers, are effectively driving higher-value transactions.

Customer Lifetime Value (CLV)

Customer Lifetime Value (CLV) is a metric that predicts the total revenue a business can expect from a customer over the course of their relationship. CLV is an important KPI for CRM because it highlights how well the company is cultivating long-term, profitable relationships with customers. A high CLV indicates that CRM initiatives are successful in driving customer retention, repeat purchases, and brand loyalty.

Customer Satisfaction and Retention KPIs

Customer satisfaction and retention are two critical components of CRM success. While CRM systems can help acquire new customers, they are even more powerful when used to nurture and retain existing customers. A loyal customer base is not only more cost-effective to maintain but also a powerful source of repeat business and referrals.

Customer Satisfaction Score (CSAT)

The Customer Satisfaction Score (CSAT) is a direct measure of how satisfied customers are with their experiences with a business. Typically, CSAT is measured through post-interaction surveys that ask customers to rate their experience. A high CSAT score indicates that the CRM system is facilitating smooth, positive interactions, and that the business is meeting or exceeding customer expectations. This metric is particularly valuable for assessing the success of customer service efforts and personalized communications.

Net Promoter Score (NPS)

Net Promoter Score (NPS) is another important KPI for measuring customer loyalty and satisfaction. NPS asks customers how likely they are to recommend a company's product or service to others, which can be an indicator of overall satisfaction. NPS is valuable because it provides insights into customer sentiment and loyalty, which are essential factors in measuring CRM success. A high NPS suggests that the CRM system is fostering strong relationships that drive customer advocacy.

Customer Retention Rate

The customer retention rate measures the percentage of customers who continue to do business with a company over a specific period of time. CRM systems are designed to enhance customer retention by providing personalized communication, targeted offers, and efficient service. A high retention rate indicates that the CRM system is effectively managing ongoing customer relationships, leading to repeat business and long-term loyalty.

Churn Rate

The churn rate measures the percentage of customers who stop doing business with a company within a given period. A low churn rate is an indicator that CRM strategies are working to maintain customer loyalty and satisfaction. By analyzing churn rates, businesses can identify potential weaknesses in their CRM efforts, such as poor customer service or ineffective communication, that may be contributing to customer attrition.

Customer Service and Support KPIs

CRM systems are critical in supporting customer service teams by providing them with the tools and data they need to resolve customer issues quickly and effectively. Measuring the performance of customer service teams is another key aspect of CRM success, as the quality of service directly influences customer satisfaction and retention.

First Response Time (FRT)

First Response Time (FRT) measures the time it takes for a customer to receive an initial response after contacting customer support. A low FRT indicates that the CRM system is streamlining the process of triaging support tickets and assigning them to the appropriate team members. Quick response times are crucial for customer satisfaction, as they signal that the company values the customer's time and is committed to resolving issues promptly.

Resolution Time

Resolution time measures the amount of time it takes to resolve a customer issue from the moment the support ticket is opened. Shorter resolution times indicate that the CRM system is providing customer service representatives with the necessary information and resources to address customer concerns efficiently. By tracking resolution time, businesses can assess whether their CRM system is contributing to faster issue resolution and improved customer satisfaction.

Case Escalation Rate

The case escalation rate measures the percentage of customer service issues that require escalation to a higher level of support. A low escalation rate suggests that the CRM system is equipping customer service representatives with the tools and knowledge they need to resolve issues independently. Conversely, a high escalation rate may indicate that the CRM system is not providing enough support or that customer service representatives require additional training or resources.

Operational Efficiency and CRM Process KPIs

CRM systems also contribute to operational efficiency by automating various processes, improving data accuracy, and enabling better collaboration across teams. Measuring the efficiency of these processes is essential for understanding the broader impact of CRM on the organization.

Data Accuracy and Completeness

Accurate, complete data is crucial for effective CRM. The more accurate the customer information, the better the CRM system can serve both the customer and the business. Measuring data accuracy and completeness involves assessing the percentage of customer records that are up-to-date and contain all the necessary information. High data accuracy enables more precise targeting of marketing campaigns, better customer service, and improved sales forecasting.

System Adoption Rate

The system adoption rate measures the percentage of employees who are actively using the CRM system to manage customer interactions. High adoption rates suggest that the CRM system is intuitive, user-friendly, and integrated effectively into business operations. Low adoption rates may indicate that the system is too complex, lacks necessary features, or is not aligned with user needs.

CRM Utilization Rate

The CRM utilization rate measures how often the features and functionalities of the CRM system are being used by employees. A high utilization rate indicates that employees are making full use of the CRM system's capabilities, leading to more efficient processes, better customer insights, and improved business outcomes. Low utilization rates may signal that employees are not fully trained on the system or that it is not meeting their needs.

Conclusion

Measuring the success of a CRM system is essential for ensuring that customer relationship strategies are delivering the desired results. By identifying and tracking the right KPIs and metrics, businesses can evaluate CRM performance across various areas such as sales growth, customer satisfaction, retention, service quality, and operational efficiency. Regularly measuring and analyzing these indicators enables organizations to make data-driven decisions, refine their CRM strategies, and ultimately enhance their customer relationships. In doing so, businesses can achieve sustained growth, improved customer loyalty, and a competitive edge in their industry.

Part 3: Optimizing Supplier Relationships with SRM

11. Supplier Segmentation and Evaluation: Identifying Strategic Partners

Supplier Relationship Management (SRM) has become a cornerstone of modern procurement strategies, with organizations recognizing the pivotal role suppliers play in their overall business performance. As businesses continue to evolve and face increasingly complex markets, having a robust SRM strategy in place is no longer optional but essential. Central to a successful SRM strategy is the concept of supplier segmentation and evaluation. These processes allow organizations to categorize suppliers based on their strategic importance and assess their performance effectively. By segmenting and evaluating suppliers, businesses can identify their most valuable partners and build long-term relationships that drive mutual benefits.

In this chapter, we will explore the importance of supplier segmentation and evaluation, the methods for identifying strategic partners, and how these practices can contribute to the optimization of supplier relationships. We will also discuss how companies can use data, metrics, and a structured approach to assess supplier performance and make informed decisions about how to engage with them.

The Need for Supplier Segmentation

Supplier segmentation is the process of classifying suppliers into different groups based on criteria such as their strategic importance, value to the business, risk levels, and performance capabilities. The objective is to create a tailored approach for managing each supplier, recognizing that not all suppliers are created equal in terms of the value they provide to the organization. By segmenting suppliers, businesses can allocate resources more effectively, build stronger relationships with key suppliers, and optimize their procurement strategies.

The need for supplier segmentation arises from the increasing complexity of supply chains. Businesses often work with a wide range of suppliers, from critical, high-value partners to low-risk, low-value vendors. Trying to treat all suppliers equally can lead to inefficiencies, missed opportunities, and strained relationships. Instead, segmentation helps organizations focus their attention and resources on those suppliers that contribute the most to the success of their business. It also ensures that businesses can manage potential risks more effectively by understanding which suppliers have the highest impact on operations and performance.

Key Criteria for Supplier Segmentation

Supplier segmentation is not a one-size-fits-all process. The criteria used for segmentation will vary depending on the specific needs of the business and the nature of its industry. However, there are several key factors that are commonly used to segment suppliers:

Strategic Importance

Strategic importance refers to the value a supplier brings to the organization's long-term success. Suppliers that provide key raw materials, technologies, or services that are essential for the organization's core operations are considered strategically important. These suppliers have a significant impact on the company's competitiveness and innovation capabilities. They are often the focus of long-term partnerships and require careful management to ensure a mutually beneficial relationship.

Volume and Spend

Volume and spend are critical factors when assessing suppliers. Suppliers that account for a high percentage of total spend or provide high-volume products and services are essential to the business. These suppliers often have a more significant impact on profitability and cost control. Businesses may choose to negotiate long-term contracts, implement price-locking strategies, or establish collaborative relationships with these suppliers to optimize cost management.

Risk

Risk assessment is another important factor in supplier segmentation. The level of risk associated with a supplier can be influenced by various factors, such as financial stability, geopolitical risks, market volatility, and regulatory compliance. High-risk suppliers may require more monitoring and mitigation strategies, such as contingency planning, diversification of suppliers, or creating alternative sourcing strategies. On the other hand, low-risk suppliers may be managed with a more hands-off approach.

Innovation Potential

Innovation is a key driver of business growth and competitive advantage. Suppliers that offer new technologies, solutions, or ideas that can enhance the company's products or services should be considered strategically important. These suppliers are often seen as partners in innovation, contributing to the company's ability to stay ahead of competitors. Collaboration with such suppliers is critical, as it can lead to product improvements, cost reductions, and access to emerging markets.

Operational Performance and Reliability

A supplier's ability to meet quality standards, deliver products on time, and fulfill orders consistently is essential for ensuring smooth operations. Suppliers that demonstrate high levels of operational performance and reliability can help businesses reduce lead times, manage inventory more effectively, and avoid production delays. Suppliers with inconsistent performance or reliability issues, however, can disrupt operations and damage customer relationships.

The Supplier Evaluation Process

Supplier evaluation is the process of assessing a supplier's performance based on established criteria to ensure they are meeting business needs and expectations. This process helps businesses determine whether a supplier is delivering on its commitments and whether it is still the right partner for the organization. Supplier evaluation typically involves both quantitative and qualitative assessments, with data-driven metrics and performance reviews playing a central role.

Supplier evaluation can be broken down into several key steps:

Defining Evaluation Criteria

Before evaluating suppliers, it is essential to establish clear evaluation criteria that align with the organization's strategic goals. The criteria should be based on the factors discussed earlier, such as strategic importance, spend, risk, innovation, and performance. For example, an evaluation criterion might include timely delivery, product quality, pricing competitiveness, or the supplier's ability to innovate. The selection of criteria should be tailored to the specific needs of the business, as different suppliers will contribute in different ways.

Collecting Data and Performance Metrics

To evaluate supplier performance effectively, businesses need to collect data on key performance metrics. These metrics can be both operational (e.g., on-time delivery, quality defect rates) and strategic (e.g., cost competitiveness, innovation potential). The data should be gathered from multiple sources, including internal teams, customer feedback, and supplier self-assessments. For example, sales teams can provide input on the quality and timeliness of product deliveries, while the procurement team can assess pricing and contract terms.

The use of digital tools and analytics platforms can simplify data collection and provide more accurate insights. CRM systems, procurement software, and data analytics platforms can offer real-time dashboards that track supplier performance across multiple metrics. This enables businesses to continuously monitor supplier relationships and make data-driven decisions based on up-to-date information.

Supplier Rating Systems

A supplier rating system can be an effective way to quantify supplier performance and compare suppliers objectively. The rating system assigns numerical scores or rankings to various evaluation criteria, such as delivery reliability, product quality, pricing, customer service, and innovation. Each criterion is weighted according to its importance, and suppliers are rated on a scale (e.g., 1 to 5, or 1 to 10) for each factor. The overall score provides a comprehensive picture of a supplier's performance and can help businesses identify strengths and areas for improvement.

Regular Performance Reviews

Supplier evaluations should be conducted regularly to ensure that supplier relationships remain aligned with business goals. These reviews can be quarterly, semi-annual, or annual, depending on the nature of the supplier relationship. During these reviews, businesses should provide feedback to suppliers, highlight areas of improvement, and discuss any concerns or challenges. It is also an opportunity to recognize and reward suppliers that demonstrate exceptional performance. Regular reviews help ensure that supplier relationships remain dynamic and responsive to changing business needs.

Identifying Strategic Partners

Not all suppliers are created equal, and businesses must identify those suppliers that play a critical role in driving long-term success. Strategic partners are those suppliers that contribute significantly to the business's competitive advantage, operational efficiency, and innovation. They are often seen as collaborators rather than mere vendors. Identifying strategic partners requires a deep understanding of the supplier base and careful consideration of the factors that define a strong partnership.

Supplier Development and Collaboration

Strategic partners often engage in joint development efforts to create value for both parties. Supplier development initiatives may include working together to improve product quality, reduce costs, or innovate new solutions. Collaboration between businesses and strategic suppliers can lead to better design, faster time-to-market, and enhanced customer experiences. Companies that identify strategic suppliers and work closely with them can achieve significant competitive advantages in their industry.

Long-Term Relationships and Contracts

Strategic partnerships are typically built on long-term, mutually beneficial agreements. These relationships are characterized by shared goals, trust, and ongoing collaboration. Long-term contracts with strategic suppliers help create stability and ensure that both parties are aligned in their objectives. A strategic supplier is willing to invest in the partnership by offering preferential terms, providing innovation, and committing to high levels of service and performance.

Innovation and Market Expansion
Strategic suppliers are often key players in a company's innovation efforts. These suppliers bring new technologies, processes, and products to the table, helping the business stay ahead of competitors. Additionally, strategic suppliers may offer access to new markets or global networks, enabling the company to expand its reach and tap into new customer segments. Identifying suppliers with strong innovation capabilities is crucial for maintaining a competitive edge in today's rapidly changing business environment.

Supplier segmentation and evaluation are essential components of an effective SRM strategy. By segmenting suppliers according to their strategic importance and performance, businesses can prioritize resources, reduce risks, and optimize supplier relationships. The evaluation process, which involves defining criteria, collecting performance data, and regularly reviewing supplier performance, helps organizations identify their most valuable partners. Building long-term relationships with these strategic suppliers fosters collaboration, innovation, and shared success. Ultimately, effective supplier segmentation and evaluation ensure that businesses can manage their supply chains efficiently, drive value from supplier relationships, and gain a competitive advantage in their industry.

12. Building Supplier Partnerships: Collaboration for Innovation and Growth

In today's fast-paced business environment, the value of suppliers goes beyond the traditional transactional relationship of merely providing goods or services. Instead, successful businesses are increasingly recognizing the importance of forging strong, long-term partnerships with their suppliers, focusing on collaboration that drives innovation and growth. This evolution of supplier relationships has become an integral part of the broader concept of Supplier Relationship Management (SRM), which prioritizes mutual benefits, strategic alignment, and joint development. For businesses aiming to gain a competitive edge, building supplier partnerships is not only about ensuring supply chain efficiency but also about fostering a collaborative ecosystem where both parties contribute to shared success.

At the heart of supplier partnerships lies the understanding that innovation is not confined to an organization's internal boundaries but often flourishes through collaboration with external partners. Suppliers are key players in a business's ability to innovate, adapt, and stay ahead of the competition. In this chapter, we explore the importance of building supplier partnerships, the key elements of a successful partnership, and how collaboration with suppliers can lead to innovation and sustained growth.

The Changing Nature of Supplier Relationships

Historically, suppliers were viewed as external entities whose role was to fulfill orders, maintain inventory levels, and adhere to contractual terms. These relationships were transactional, and the primary focus was on cost reduction, delivery schedules, and product quality. While these elements remain important, the dynamics of global business and rapidly evolving markets have shifted the way companies view their suppliers.

With increasing competition, shorter product life cycles, and the constant pressure to innovate, companies have realized that their suppliers can be more than just providers of goods and services.

Suppliers can be critical enablers of innovation, cost management, and market expansion. As such, forward-thinking organizations have begun to view suppliers as strategic partners, engaging with them as collaborators to co-create value, explore new opportunities, and drive business growth. This shift has led to the rise of supplier partnership models, which focus on creating long-term, mutually beneficial relationships, rather than short-term, transactional engagements.

The Importance of Collaboration in Supplier Partnerships

Collaboration is the cornerstone of any successful supplier partnership. It goes beyond simply managing transactions to creating an environment where both parties work together to achieve common goals. This collaboration is based on trust, transparency, and shared objectives, and it encourages suppliers to become more involved in the decision-making processes of the business.

When suppliers are seen as strategic partners rather than just vendors, the potential for joint innovation increases. Suppliers often have unique expertise in specific areas, whether it be technology, materials, or manufacturing processes. By involving suppliers early in the development stages of products or services, companies can tap into this expertise to create more efficient processes, higher quality products, or new solutions that wouldn't be possible with a traditional, arms-length supplier relationship.

Collaboration also helps businesses manage risks more effectively. In a partnership model, suppliers are often more willing to share critical information, such as market trends, production challenges, or supply chain disruptions. This open communication allows businesses to anticipate and mitigate risks together, rather than responding reactively when problems arise.

Key Elements of a Successful Supplier Partnership

Building successful supplier partnerships requires a strategic, well-thought-out approach that involves several key elements. These elements are the foundation upon which long-term, collaborative relationships are built, and they help create the conditions necessary for innovation and growth.

Trust and Transparency
Trust is the bedrock of any successful partnership. Without trust, collaboration is difficult, if not impossible. For trust to flourish, both parties must demonstrate transparency in their operations, share information freely, and engage in open communication. Trust is built over time, and it requires both parties to be honest about their capabilities, challenges, and expectations. Suppliers should feel confident that their business partners will support them in meeting mutual goals, while companies must trust their suppliers to deliver on promises.

Transparency goes hand in hand with trust. When both parties share information, whether it's related to production schedules, quality metrics, or financial data, it creates an environment where decisions can be made based on a clear understanding of the situation. This transparency also fosters accountability, ensuring that both sides are committed to achieving the desired outcomes.

Clear Communication
Clear communication is another essential element of successful supplier partnerships. Without effective communication, misunderstandings, inefficiencies, and delays can easily arise. Businesses and suppliers must set up regular channels for communication to discuss ongoing projects, address issues, and align on goals. Communication should not be limited to formal meetings but should be an ongoing process that includes sharing updates, feedback, and any potential changes to expectations or priorities.

Open and frequent communication helps prevent issues from escalating and ensures that both parties are aligned on key objectives. Whether it's discussing product specifications, timelines, or potential roadblocks, frequent dialogue is necessary to keep the partnership on track and address any concerns promptly.

Shared Goals and Objectives

A successful supplier partnership is driven by shared goals. Both the business and the supplier must be aligned in terms of what they hope to achieve from the relationship. This alignment is critical because it ensures that both parties are working towards the same objectives and that their efforts are complementary rather than conflicting. Shared goals also foster collaboration because both sides recognize that their success is intertwined.

In setting shared goals, it's important for businesses to involve suppliers early in the process. By clearly outlining what is expected from each party and ensuring that the goals are realistic and achievable, both sides can commit to working together toward success. Goals should be specific, measurable, and aligned with the overall strategic direction of the business, and they should be regularly reviewed and updated to reflect any changes in the business environment.

Mutual Benefits

One of the key characteristics of a successful supplier partnership is the emphasis on mutual benefits. In a transactional relationship, the focus is often on maximizing one party's benefit at the expense of the other. In contrast, a partnership aims to create value for both sides. This value can take various forms, such as improved profitability, reduced costs, or enhanced product quality. The key is that both parties see tangible benefits from the partnership, which reinforces the commitment to the relationship.

For instance, suppliers that collaborate on product development may benefit from improved manufacturing processes, while the business gains access to innovative products or services. Similarly, businesses that share insights into consumer trends or market demands can help suppliers adapt and expand their offerings. By ensuring that both sides benefit from the partnership, companies can create long-lasting relationships that drive sustained growth.

Innovation and Continuous Improvement

At the heart of supplier partnerships is the drive for innovation.

Suppliers who are deeply engaged in the development process can contribute valuable insights into how products can be improved or how processes can be optimized. By working closely with suppliers, businesses can leverage their expertise to develop new technologies, streamline operations, and create products that meet the evolving needs of customers.

Innovation in supplier partnerships is not limited to product development. It also extends to process improvements, cost reduction strategies, and supply chain efficiency. Suppliers can help businesses identify opportunities for automation, optimize inventory management, or reduce lead times. By fostering a culture of continuous improvement, businesses and suppliers can keep pushing the boundaries of what is possible, driving long-term growth and competitiveness.

Risk Management and Resilience

In today's complex global supply chains, risk management is critical. A strong supplier partnership can help businesses navigate uncertainties by creating a more resilient supply chain. When suppliers and businesses work together closely, they can identify potential risks early, develop contingency plans, and implement strategies to mitigate those risks.

For example, by sharing forecasts and production schedules, suppliers can better anticipate demand fluctuations and adjust their operations accordingly. Additionally, businesses and suppliers can collaborate to identify alternative sources of raw materials or logistics options in the event of supply disruptions. By building resilience into their relationships, companies and suppliers can ensure that their supply chains remain robust even in the face of challenges.

The Role of Technology in Supplier Partnerships

Technology plays a crucial role in enabling and enhancing supplier partnerships. From the use of data analytics to cloud-based collaboration platforms, technology can streamline communication, improve transparency, and foster innovation. Many organizations are leveraging digital tools to manage their supplier relationships more effectively, using software to track performance, share data, and collaborate on product development.

For instance, cloud-based platforms allow businesses and suppliers to share documents, access real-time data, and collaborate seamlessly across geographies. Similarly, predictive analytics tools enable businesses to forecast demand, identify trends, and make data-driven decisions in partnership with their suppliers. By integrating technology into their supplier relationships, companies can enhance collaboration, reduce friction, and unlock new opportunities for growth.

Conclusion

Building supplier partnerships is a strategic approach that drives innovation, growth, and competitive advantage. By focusing on collaboration, trust, transparency, and shared goals, businesses can forge long-term relationships with suppliers that go beyond simple transactions. Supplier partnerships enable companies to tap into the expertise and capabilities of their suppliers, driving mutual benefits and fostering a culture of continuous improvement. In today's fast-evolving business landscape, companies that prioritize supplier collaboration are better positioned to adapt, innovate, and thrive. Through these partnerships, businesses and suppliers can work together to navigate challenges, seize new opportunities, and ultimately achieve sustained growth.

13. Technology in SRM: From e-Procurement to Blockchain Applications

Supplier Relationship Management (SRM) has undergone a significant transformation over the past decade. With advancements in technology, businesses are now able to streamline, optimize, and innovate their supplier interactions in ways that were previously unimaginable. As organizations seek to build stronger, more efficient, and more transparent relationships with their suppliers, technology has become a critical enabler of these goals. From e-procurement platforms that simplify the purchasing process to the advent of blockchain, which promises to revolutionize transparency and trust in supply chains, the role of technology in SRM cannot be overstated.

In this chapter, we explore how technology has reshaped SRM practices, from early-stage e-procurement systems to more sophisticated blockchain applications that promise to reshape the way businesses interact with their suppliers. We will also examine the role of data analytics, automation, and artificial intelligence (AI) in modernizing SRM, enhancing supplier collaboration, and ensuring smoother, more cost-effective supply chain management.

The Evolution of Technology in SRM

The evolution of technology in SRM is closely tied to the increasing need for efficiency, transparency, and real-time decision-making. Over the years, businesses have recognized that traditional supplier management approaches were no longer sufficient in an increasingly globalized and fast-paced business environment. The first wave of technological advancement in SRM was marked by the adoption of e-procurement systems, which allowed companies to automate and digitize their procurement processes.

E-Procurement Systems

E-procurement systems, which include supplier portals, electronic purchase orders, and invoice management, were developed to streamline the procurement process by digitizing and automating key tasks. These systems replaced the manual, paper-based processes that were prone to errors and inefficiencies. By automating routine tasks such as order placement, invoice processing, and supplier communications, e-procurement platforms enabled businesses to improve procurement accuracy, reduce costs, and accelerate transaction cycles.

Moreover, e-procurement platforms provided a central repository for supplier information, making it easier for procurement teams to manage and track supplier performance. These platforms also facilitated communication between suppliers and buyers, allowing for better collaboration and quicker decision-making. As a result, e-procurement systems laid the foundation for more advanced supplier relationship management practices, providing businesses with a more structured, data-driven approach to managing their suppliers.

The next wave of technological evolution saw the introduction of advanced analytics and AI, which allowed businesses to further optimize their supplier relationships by leveraging large volumes of data. These technologies enabled companies to better assess supplier performance, predict potential risks, and make more informed decisions regarding supplier selection, contract management, and ongoing relationships.

The Role of Artificial Intelligence in SRM

Artificial intelligence (AI) has played a transformative role in SRM by enabling companies to automate complex tasks, analyze vast amounts of data, and predict future outcomes. AI tools can identify patterns in supplier behavior, forecast demand, and provide valuable insights into supplier performance, helping organizations make more informed decisions about their supplier base.

AI-driven analytics can provide predictive insights that help businesses anticipate potential issues, such as delivery delays, quality problems, or changes in supplier capacity. These predictive models allow businesses to proactively address problems before they escalate, thereby reducing the risk of supply chain disruptions. For example, AI-powered algorithms can analyze historical data to identify trends in supplier performance, such as frequent delays in delivery or issues with product quality, and offer recommendations on how to mitigate these risks in the future.

Another area where AI is making a significant impact is in supplier segmentation and selection. Traditional supplier evaluation methods often rely on historical performance data, but AI can go beyond this by analyzing multiple data points, such as market conditions, geopolitical risks, and supplier financial health, to provide a more comprehensive view of a potential supplier's suitability. This allows businesses to make smarter, data-driven decisions when selecting suppliers, ultimately improving supplier quality and performance.

AI is also playing a critical role in contract management. By using natural language processing (NLP) algorithms, AI tools can analyze and extract key terms from contracts, ensuring that businesses are compliant with contractual agreements and reducing the risk of disputes. These tools can automatically flag any deviations from the agreed terms, ensuring that suppliers meet their obligations and making it easier for procurement teams to manage multiple contracts simultaneously.

Blockchain in SRM: Revolutionizing Transparency and Trust

One of the most exciting technological advancements in SRM in recent years has been the emergence of blockchain technology. Blockchain, best known for its role in cryptocurrency, has the potential to revolutionize how businesses manage their relationships with suppliers by providing an immutable, transparent, and decentralized ledger of transactions.

At its core, blockchain technology provides a secure, transparent, and tamper-proof way of recording transactions. Each transaction is recorded as a "block" on the blockchain, which is linked to the previous block, creating an unalterable chain of data. This feature makes blockchain an ideal tool for managing supplier transactions, as it ensures that all parties involved in a transaction have access to the same data and can track every step of the process.

In the context of SRM, blockchain can be used to increase transparency, improve traceability, and reduce the risk of fraud. For example, blockchain can be used to track the provenance of raw materials or products, ensuring that they come from ethical and sustainable sources. This is particularly important in industries such as food, pharmaceuticals, and luxury goods, where consumers and regulators demand high levels of transparency regarding product sourcing.

Moreover, blockchain's ability to create smart contracts—self-executing contracts with the terms of the agreement directly written into the code—has the potential to revolutionize how businesses and suppliers interact. Smart contracts can automatically execute actions when predefined conditions are met, reducing the need for manual intervention and ensuring that agreements are upheld without the risk of human error. For instance, a smart contract could automatically release payment to a supplier once the agreed-upon terms, such as product delivery or quality standards, are met. This reduces the risk of disputes and ensures faster, more reliable transactions.

Additionally, blockchain can be used to streamline the procurement process by providing a secure, transparent platform for all parties involved. By allowing businesses and suppliers to track and verify every stage of the procurement cycle, blockchain technology reduces the risk of fraud, errors, and delays. The decentralized nature of blockchain also makes it easier for businesses to collaborate with multiple suppliers across different geographies, as all parties can access the same data in real-time, ensuring consistency and transparency.

The Integration of Technology in SRM

The integration of technology in SRM is not just about adopting individual tools but creating a cohesive, interconnected ecosystem of systems that work together seamlessly. In modern SRM, this often involves the integration of e-procurement platforms, AI tools, blockchain applications, and other technologies to create a holistic solution for managing supplier relationships.

For example, a business may use e-procurement platforms to streamline the ordering process, AI-powered analytics to assess supplier performance, and blockchain to track the provenance of products and ensure transparency in the supply chain. By integrating these technologies, businesses can create a more efficient, agile, and resilient supplier relationship management system that is capable of responding quickly to changing market conditions and supply chain disruptions.

The integration of these technologies also enables businesses to gain real-time insights into their supplier relationships. With AI tools analyzing supplier performance data, blockchain providing a transparent view of transactions, and e-procurement platforms automating routine tasks, businesses can make more informed decisions about their supplier base. These insights enable companies to proactively manage their suppliers, identify opportunities for collaboration and innovation, and mitigate risks before they become problems.

The Future of Technology in SRM

As technology continues to evolve, the potential applications for SRM will only expand. The rise of the Internet of Things (IoT) is set to further transform supplier relationships by enabling real-time tracking of goods and materials, providing businesses with greater visibility into their supply chains. Similarly, advancements in data analytics and AI will enable businesses to gain even deeper insights into supplier performance, enabling more targeted and effective supplier management strategies.

Furthermore, the increasing use of cloud-based platforms for SRM is expected to enhance collaboration between businesses and their suppliers, enabling them to share data and communicate more efficiently. Cloud platforms allow businesses and suppliers to access real-time information from anywhere in the world, fostering greater flexibility and responsiveness.

Blockchain technology, too, will continue to evolve and find new applications in SRM. As the technology matures, it is likely that businesses will increasingly adopt blockchain-based solutions for contract management, payments, and supply chain traceability, further enhancing transparency, trust, and efficiency in supplier relationships.

Conclusion

Technology has become an indispensable tool in modern Supplier Relationship Management, enabling businesses to streamline processes, enhance collaboration, and drive innovation. From the early days of e-procurement systems to the transformative potential of blockchain, technology is reshaping the way businesses interact with their suppliers. As businesses continue to embrace advanced technologies such as AI, IoT, and blockchain, they will be better positioned to build stronger, more strategic supplier relationships that drive growth, mitigate risk, and ensure long-term success. The future of SRM lies in the integration of these technologies, which will create more agile, resilient, and transparent supply chains that are capable of responding to the challenges of an ever-changing global marketplace.

14. Managing Supplier Risks: Mitigating Disruptions in the Supply Chain

In today's interconnected and globalized business environment, the ability to manage supplier risks is a critical competency for businesses striving to maintain operational efficiency, protect their reputation, and safeguard their bottom line. Supply chains are inherently complex, involving multiple suppliers from different regions, industries, and business cultures. This complexity, while presenting opportunities for cost-saving and innovation, also exposes businesses to a range of risks that can disrupt operations, compromise product quality, and delay delivery timelines. Whether due to natural disasters, geopolitical issues, financial instability, or supplier mismanagement, the potential for supply chain disruptions is ever-present.

Effective supplier risk management involves identifying, assessing, and mitigating these risks before they escalate into significant problems. By proactively managing risks, businesses can strengthen supplier relationships, reduce the likelihood of disruptions, and ensure continuity in the supply chain. This chapter explores various types of supplier risks, methods for assessing and mitigating these risks, and strategies for building a more resilient supply chain.

The Importance of Supplier Risk Management

Risk management in supply chains is not just about reacting to problems as they arise; it's about creating an environment where risks are anticipated, prepared for, and mitigated before they can cause significant damage. A well-managed supplier risk management system can help businesses maintain continuity of operations, preserve customer trust, and avoid costly disruptions. A failure to properly manage supplier risks can lead to delayed deliveries, compromised product quality, reputational damage, and, in the worst cases, loss of market position.

Additionally, suppliers themselves can present risks in various forms. Financial instability, poor production processes, geopolitical instability in the supplier's region, environmental factors, and technological vulnerabilities all represent potential disruptions. Addressing these risks requires a holistic approach that combines proactive risk identification with real-time monitoring, collaboration with suppliers, and the use of technology to optimize risk management processes.

Types of Supplier Risks

Supplier risks are diverse and multifaceted. Identifying the specific types of risks is the first step in developing effective risk management strategies. Broadly, supplier risks can be categorized into several key areas:

Operational Risks

Operational risks in the context of supplier relationships relate to the supplier's ability to meet agreed-upon standards of production and delivery. These risks could arise from factors such as poor quality control, breakdowns in manufacturing processes, or failure to meet product specifications. Supplier capacity issues, such as labor shortages or equipment failure, can also lead to operational risks. Businesses must ensure that suppliers have the necessary infrastructure and resources to meet demand and maintain quality standards.

Financial Risks

Financial instability or poor financial health of suppliers is another significant risk in supplier management. A supplier facing cash flow issues or operating with a high level of debt may struggle to fulfill its obligations or could go out of business altogether, leading to disruption in the supply chain. Assessing the financial stability of key suppliers should be a core element of any risk management strategy. This can involve analyzing financial statements, credit ratings, and other indicators of financial health.

Geopolitical and Regulatory Risks

Geopolitical risks stem from factors such as political instability, changes in government regulations, tariffs, sanctions, or civil unrest in a supplier's country or region. Trade wars, regulatory changes, or shifts in government policies can disrupt the supply chain, making it difficult or expensive to source materials or deliver products. Businesses should actively monitor geopolitical developments and regulatory changes that may impact their suppliers. Diversification of the supplier base, including sourcing from multiple regions, can mitigate the effects of these risks.

Natural and Environmental Risks

Environmental factors, including natural disasters, climate change, and pandemics, pose considerable risks to suppliers. Natural events like floods, earthquakes, hurricanes, and wildfires can disrupt production, transportation, and logistics, while the effects of climate change—such as rising sea levels or more frequent extreme weather events—can have long-term consequences on supplier operations. Companies must assess the environmental risks associated with their supply chain and develop contingency plans to minimize disruption from these events. Building resilient supply chains requires considering these risks when selecting suppliers, especially in regions prone to natural disasters.

Technological Risks

The increasing reliance on technology and digital systems in the supply chain introduces technological risks. Cybersecurity threats, data breaches, system failures, and reliance on outdated software or hardware can all cause supply chain disruptions. For example, a cyber-attack on a supplier's system could compromise product designs or disrupt operations, while an IT system failure could delay order processing and shipments. To mitigate these risks, businesses should conduct regular cybersecurity assessments, ensure that suppliers adhere to industry standards for data protection, and invest in robust IT infrastructure that supports supply chain operations.

Compliance Risks

Compliance with legal, ethical, and regulatory standards is critical in today's business environment. A supplier's failure to adhere to laws regarding labor practices, environmental impact, product safety, or intellectual property can result in legal and reputational risks for the business. Non-compliance can lead to fines, lawsuits, and damage to the company's brand image. Regular audits, third-party inspections, and due diligence on suppliers can help ensure that they meet compliance requirements and align with the company's ethical standards.

Assessing Supplier Risks

Once the different types of supplier risks have been identified, the next step is to assess and evaluate the potential impact of these risks on the business. Risk assessment involves gathering relevant data about suppliers and analyzing it to determine the likelihood and severity of different risks.

Supplier Risk Mapping

One of the most effective ways to assess supplier risk is through supplier risk mapping. This process involves categorizing suppliers based on the risk they pose to the supply chain. Key factors for categorization might include the supplier's financial stability, geographical location, historical performance, and the criticality of the goods or services they provide. By mapping suppliers according to risk, companies can prioritize risk mitigation efforts and focus on the suppliers that represent the greatest threats to the supply chain.

Supplier Audits and Assessments

Regular audits and assessments of supplier operations provide valuable insight into potential risks. These assessments should cover areas such as quality control, production capacity, financial health, compliance with environmental standards, and adherence to regulatory requirements. Audits can be performed internally or by third-party agencies that specialize in evaluating supplier performance. The information gathered through audits should be used to inform risk management strategies, enabling companies to proactively address issues before they lead to disruptions.

Risk Scoring Systems

Another approach to assessing supplier risk is the use of a risk scoring system. This method assigns scores to various risk factors based on their potential impact on the business. For example, a supplier located in a politically unstable region might receive a higher risk score due to geopolitical risks, while a supplier with strong financial health and a history of timely deliveries might receive a low-risk score. The scores are then used to prioritize which risks need to be mitigated most urgently.

Mitigating Supplier Risks

Once risks have been identified and assessed, businesses can implement strategies to mitigate these risks and ensure that the supply chain remains resilient and operational. Risk mitigation strategies are typically proactive measures designed to reduce the likelihood of disruptions, as well as contingency plans to manage risks when they do occur.

Diversifying the Supplier Base

One of the most effective ways to mitigate supplier risk is by diversifying the supplier base. Relying too heavily on a single supplier or supplier group can create vulnerabilities in the supply chain, especially if that supplier faces financial difficulties, capacity issues, or geopolitical challenges. By spreading risk across multiple suppliers and regions, businesses can reduce the potential impact of disruptions from any single source. Supplier diversification should also include choosing suppliers with complementary capabilities, so that if one supplier faces challenges, another can step in to provide the necessary goods or services.

Building Strong Supplier Relationships

A key component of managing supplier risks is fostering strong, collaborative relationships with suppliers. Open communication, mutual trust, and a shared commitment to quality and performance are crucial for ensuring that suppliers remain reliable partners. Regular meetings, feedback loops, and joint problem-solving efforts can help identify potential risks early and ensure that both parties are prepared to address them. Strong supplier relationships also facilitate better transparency, making it easier to address issues such as delays, quality concerns, or compliance failures before they escalate into major disruptions.

Creating Contingency Plans

Despite best efforts, some risks are unavoidable. In these cases, having a contingency plan in place is essential for minimizing disruption. Contingency plans should outline the steps to be taken in the event of a supplier failure, natural disaster, or other major risk. These plans should include alternative suppliers, backup inventory, and emergency logistics strategies. The goal is to ensure that the business can continue operations with minimal downtime, even in the face of significant disruptions.

Leveraging Technology for Risk Monitoring

Technology plays a critical role in managing and mitigating supplier risks. Tools such as supply chain visibility platforms, AI-powered analytics, and blockchain can provide real-time data on supplier performance and potential risks. For example, supply chain visibility platforms allow businesses to track shipments, monitor production schedules, and identify potential delays before they affect delivery timelines. AI-powered predictive analytics can forecast risks such as demand fluctuations, material shortages, or disruptions in transportation, enabling businesses to take preemptive action.

Conclusion

Managing supplier risks is an essential component of effective supply chain management. In an increasingly volatile and interconnected world, businesses must take proactive steps to identify, assess, and mitigate risks across their supplier base. By understanding the various types of supplier risks, implementing effective risk management strategies, and leveraging technology for real-time monitoring and data-driven decision-making, businesses can reduce the likelihood of disruptions and ensure continuity in their supply chains. A resilient supply chain, built on strong supplier relationships and sound risk management practices, is a competitive advantage in the modern business landscape, helping businesses navigate uncertainty and thrive in an increasingly complex global marketplace.

15. Sustainability in SRM: Promoting Ethical and Green Supply Chains

In the modern business landscape, sustainability has become a central focus for companies striving to not only enhance their market position but also align with the evolving expectations of consumers, stakeholders, and regulators. This growing demand for sustainable practices has pushed businesses to rethink how they manage their relationships with suppliers. Supplier Relationship Management (SRM), a critical function in any organization's supply chain strategy, plays a vital role in ensuring that sustainability is embedded into the supply chain.

Sustainability in SRM focuses on the integration of ethical, environmental, and social considerations into supplier selection, evaluation, and ongoing management. A sustainable approach in SRM not only helps businesses reduce their environmental footprint but also supports broader goals related to corporate social responsibility (CSR), regulatory compliance, and long-term business viability. By promoting green and ethical supply chains, companies can create value for both themselves and society, establishing stronger relationships with suppliers, customers, and investors.

The Growing Importance of Sustainability in SRM

Sustainability in SRM is no longer just a trend but a necessity. Companies are increasingly held accountable for the environmental and social impacts of their supply chains. Factors such as climate change, resource depletion, labor conditions, and waste management are critical concerns for businesses today. Moreover, consumers and investors are paying more attention to the ethical and environmental practices of the companies they support. This shift in consumer behavior and investor sentiment has made sustainability a key differentiator in business strategies.

The ability to create a sustainable supply chain also offers long-term financial benefits. By managing resources more efficiently, reducing waste, and improving operational practices, businesses can reduce costs and enhance profitability. Sustainable practices can also help mitigate risks related to regulatory non-compliance and reputational damage. As governments around the world enact stricter environmental regulations and standards, businesses that have already adopted sustainable practices are better positioned to adapt to these changes.

Key Aspects of Sustainability in SRM

Sustainability in SRM can be broken down into several key components that span environmental, social, and economic dimensions. These components guide businesses in establishing and maintaining sustainable relationships with suppliers.

Environmental Sustainability

Environmental sustainability in SRM focuses on minimizing the negative ecological impact of supply chains. This includes reducing greenhouse gas emissions, conserving natural resources, minimizing waste, and adopting eco-friendly practices. Suppliers are evaluated based on their environmental performance, including their ability to comply with environmental regulations, use renewable energy, reduce emissions, and adopt sustainable production methods.

The concept of the circular economy, which emphasizes the reuse, recycling, and repurposing of materials, is becoming an increasingly important focus in sustainable supply chains. Businesses are working with suppliers to ensure that materials used in products can be recycled or reused at the end of their lifecycle, reducing waste and environmental degradation. Additionally, eco-friendly packaging, energy-efficient manufacturing, and low-carbon transportation are vital aspects of sustainability in SRM.

Social Sustainability

Social sustainability in SRM is concerned with ensuring that suppliers uphold ethical labor practices, human rights, and community welfare. Businesses are increasingly required to ensure that their suppliers do not engage in exploitative practices such as child labor, forced labor, or unsafe working conditions. In addition, social sustainability includes promoting fair wages, supporting diversity and inclusion, and fostering a safe and healthy working environment for all employees.

Beyond the workplace, social sustainability also involves contributing positively to the communities where suppliers operate. This can involve suppliers making efforts to improve local living conditions, providing education and skills development to workers, and engaging in charitable or community-based initiatives. By fostering ethical and socially responsible suppliers, businesses can ensure that their supply chains support the well-being of workers and local communities, while also safeguarding their reputation and long-term business interests.

Economic Sustainability

Economic sustainability focuses on the financial viability of suppliers and the long-term success of the supply chain. It ensures that suppliers are financially stable, capable of meeting the company's demand, and able to sustain their operations over time. In the context of SRM, economic sustainability is about building mutually beneficial partnerships that are not solely based on cost but also on the long-term value created by the relationship.

A key aspect of economic sustainability is fair pricing, where suppliers are paid fairly for their goods and services. Sustainable pricing allows suppliers to maintain high standards of quality, invest in their workforce, and adopt environmentally friendly practices. Businesses that engage in sustainable SRM ensure that suppliers are financially supported and incentivized to invest in more sustainable practices, which can enhance the overall resilience and competitiveness of the supply chain.

Implementing Sustainability in SRM

To promote sustainability in SRM, businesses must take a systematic approach that integrates sustainability into every stage of the supplier relationship lifecycle—from supplier selection to performance monitoring. This process involves setting clear sustainability goals, establishing criteria for supplier evaluation, and collaborating with suppliers to achieve shared sustainability objectives.

Supplier Selection and Evaluation

When selecting suppliers, businesses should assess not only their ability to meet quality and delivery standards but also their environmental and social performance. Supplier selection criteria should include factors such as the supplier's commitment to reducing their carbon footprint, their waste management practices, and their labor policies. Using sustainability as part of the supplier selection process helps companies build a supply chain that is aligned with their own values and sustainability goals.

A supplier evaluation process that incorporates sustainability criteria enables businesses to measure and track the performance of suppliers over time. This can include monitoring suppliers' adherence to environmental regulations, their ability to reduce waste, their use of renewable energy, and their labor practices. In addition to traditional supplier audits, businesses should consider conducting sustainability audits to evaluate suppliers' environmental, social, and governance (ESG) performance.

Supplier Collaboration and Development

Sustainability in SRM requires a collaborative approach between businesses and their suppliers. Building strong, long-term relationships with suppliers based on shared sustainability goals fosters innovation and continuous improvement. By working together, businesses and suppliers can identify opportunities for reducing environmental impact, improving efficiency, and driving innovation in product design and manufacturing processes.

Supplier development programs can be implemented to support suppliers in adopting more sustainable practices. This can include providing training on energy efficiency, waste reduction, and responsible sourcing. Collaboration on sustainability initiatives, such as joint environmental certifications or participation in industry-wide sustainability programs, can help suppliers improve their practices and align more closely with the buyer's sustainability objectives.

Monitoring and Reporting Sustainability Performance

Once sustainability goals are set and suppliers are selected, businesses must monitor and track their suppliers' performance to ensure that sustainability objectives are being met. Regular sustainability audits, performance reviews, and reporting mechanisms are essential for assessing progress and identifying areas for improvement.

Technology can play a key role in monitoring sustainability performance. Supply chain visibility platforms, for example, provide real-time data on suppliers' environmental and social performance, allowing businesses to track emissions, waste, and labor practices. Additionally, tools such as blockchain can be used to ensure transparency and traceability, enabling businesses to verify that suppliers are meeting sustainability standards.

Encouraging Innovation for Sustainability

Innovation plays a central role in driving sustainability in the supply chain. By encouraging suppliers to invest in research and development (R&D) focused on sustainability, businesses can promote the creation of new products, processes, and technologies that reduce environmental impact and improve efficiency. Suppliers that embrace innovation in areas such as green energy, sustainable materials, and circular manufacturing processes can help businesses achieve their sustainability goals while also gaining a competitive edge in the market.

Incentivizing innovation can be achieved through financial rewards, shared resources for R&D, or establishing sustainability-driven supplier awards. When suppliers are motivated to innovate in sustainability, it benefits both parties by creating new opportunities for cost savings, environmental impact reduction, and enhanced customer satisfaction.

Conclusion

Sustainability in SRM is a powerful strategy that can transform the way businesses manage their supply chains, creating long-term value while benefiting the environment, society, and the economy. By focusing on environmental responsibility, ethical labor practices, and fair economic practices, businesses can build supply chains that are not only resilient and efficient but also aligned with the values and expectations of modern consumers, investors, and regulators.

Promoting sustainability in SRM requires a holistic, collaborative approach that involves selecting, evaluating, and developing suppliers based on shared sustainability goals. It also necessitates ongoing monitoring and reporting to ensure that sustainability objectives are met. As sustainability becomes an increasingly important factor in business success, organizations that prioritize ethical and green supply chains will be better positioned to thrive in a competitive, environmentally-conscious market.

Part 4: Integrating CRM and SRM for Holistic Success

16. Unified Relationship Management: Bridging the Customer and Supplier Divide

In today's fast-paced and interconnected business world, organizations are constantly seeking ways to improve their operational efficiencies and gain competitive advantages. One of the most effective strategies for achieving this is integrating Customer Relationship Management (CRM) and Supplier Relationship Management (SRM) systems into a unified approach. By bridging the divide between customer and supplier relationships, businesses can create a more cohesive, efficient, and adaptable supply chain and customer experience, fostering stronger and more resilient business outcomes.

Historically, CRM and SRM were treated as separate functions within organizations, with little overlap in strategy or execution. CRM focused primarily on managing and nurturing customer interactions, while SRM was centered around optimizing supplier relationships to ensure a steady supply of quality goods and services. However, as customer expectations evolve, and businesses seek deeper insights into their supply chains, the need for a more integrated approach has become apparent.

A unified relationship management strategy allows companies to leverage the synergies between customer and supplier data, enabling them to make more informed decisions, enhance communication, and create a more seamless flow of information across the business. This chapter explores the importance of bridging the customer and supplier divide, the benefits of a unified relationship management approach, and the practical steps organizations can take to implement such a system effectively.

The Need for Unified Relationship Management

In a typical business environment, the functions of CRM and SRM operate in silos. CRM systems focus on understanding and managing customer needs, preferences, and feedback, while SRM systems prioritize optimizing the relationships with suppliers, ensuring quality, cost-effectiveness, and timely delivery of goods. While these two areas serve different purposes, they are both essential to an organization's overall success, and their integration can yield significant business benefits.

The need for unifying CRM and SRM arises from the interconnected nature of modern business ecosystems. Customers and suppliers are no longer isolated entities; they are part of a larger value chain that spans multiple touchpoints and processes. The experiences of customers are influenced by the performance of suppliers, and suppliers themselves are impacted by shifts in customer demand, preferences, and behavior. Therefore, organizations must break down the silos between CRM and SRM to enable smoother interactions and a more holistic view of their business relationships.

A unified relationship management system allows businesses to integrate both customer and supplier data into a single platform, providing a comprehensive understanding of the entire supply and demand cycle. This integration can enhance decision-making, improve forecasting, streamline communication, and optimize the customer and supplier experience across the value chain.

Benefits of a Unified Relationship Management Approach

By bridging the customer and supplier divide, organizations can unlock several strategic benefits that drive both operational efficiency and customer satisfaction. These benefits include:

Enhanced Communication and Collaboration

A unified CRM and SRM system fosters improved communication between internal teams, customers, and suppliers. With shared information across both functions, teams can collaborate more effectively, making it easier to resolve issues, respond to changing customer demands, and address supply chain disruptions. For example, customer service teams can access real-time data on supplier performance, allowing them to provide more accurate and timely updates to customers. Similarly, procurement teams can gain insights into customer preferences and demand trends, enabling them to work with suppliers to anticipate future needs.

Improved Customer and Supplier Experience

When customers and suppliers are viewed as interconnected elements of a value chain, their experiences can be better managed. A unified approach allows businesses to anticipate and address customer needs while ensuring suppliers are prepared to meet these demands. For instance, by sharing insights from customer feedback and purchasing behavior with suppliers, businesses can work together to create products that meet customer expectations and improve product quality. Similarly, by understanding supplier constraints and capabilities, customer service teams can better manage customer expectations and provide more accurate delivery timelines.

Better Decision-Making and Forecasting

Integrating CRM and SRM systems provides businesses with a more complete view of the market and operational environment. By combining customer data (such as purchasing behavior and demand forecasts) with supplier data (such as lead times and inventory levels), companies can make better-informed decisions about production, procurement, and inventory management. This unified data allows organizations to optimize resource allocation, reduce inventory costs, and improve demand forecasting. Additionally, understanding the interdependencies between customer demand and supplier capabilities can help businesses proactively address potential bottlenecks or disruptions in the supply chain.

Streamlined Processes and Efficiency

The integration of CRM and SRM can lead to greater process efficiency across the organization. Instead of having separate systems for managing customer relationships and supplier interactions, businesses can centralize their processes, reducing the need for duplicate data entry, manual coordination, and cross-functional silos. This streamlined approach can result in faster response times, reduced operational costs, and improved overall efficiency.

Strengthened Strategic Partnerships

A unified relationship management system fosters stronger, more collaborative relationships with both customers and suppliers. By sharing data and insights across both functions, businesses can identify opportunities for innovation, co-development, and mutual growth. Suppliers can gain a better understanding of customer demands and expectations, enabling them to offer solutions that are more closely aligned with market needs. Similarly, businesses can gain deeper insights into supplier capabilities and constraints, allowing for more strategic and long-term partnerships.

Practical Steps to Implement Unified Relationship Management

To realize the benefits of a unified CRM and SRM approach, businesses need to take several practical steps to integrate their systems, processes, and teams. The following steps outline a roadmap for implementing unified relationship management effectively:

1. Establish Clear Objectives and Goals

Before integrating CRM and SRM systems, it is essential for businesses to define the objectives and goals they wish to achieve. These could include improving customer satisfaction, reducing supply chain disruptions, enhancing collaboration with suppliers, or optimizing demand forecasting. Having clear, measurable objectives ensures that the integration process stays focused and aligned with the company's strategic priorities.

2. Integrate Data and Systems

The foundation of unified relationship management is the seamless integration of customer and supplier data. Businesses should ensure that their CRM and SRM systems are compatible or that they use a centralized platform that can house both sets of data. Data integration should involve standardizing data formats, ensuring data accuracy, and establishing systems for data sharing between departments. This integration should also extend to any other relevant business systems (such as enterprise resource planning, or ERP systems) to ensure that all teams have access to the same information.

3. Foster Cross-Functional Collaboration

A unified relationship management approach requires collaboration across different departments, including sales, procurement, customer service, and supply chain management. Teams must be aligned in their understanding of customer and supplier needs and be committed to working together to achieve common goals. Regular cross-functional meetings, joint planning sessions, and shared performance metrics can help facilitate this collaboration and ensure that both customer and supplier relationships are managed effectively.

4. Leverage Technology for Automation and Analytics

Advanced technologies such as artificial intelligence (AI), machine learning, and data analytics can play a significant role in optimizing unified relationship management. These technologies can help automate routine tasks, provide real-time insights, and identify patterns in customer behavior and supplier performance. For example, AI-powered analytics can predict customer demand based on historical data and supply chain trends, while machine learning algorithms can optimize supplier selection and inventory management. By leveraging these technologies, businesses can enhance the efficiency and effectiveness of their unified CRM and SRM approach.

5. Monitor and Continuously Improve

Once the unified relationship management system is in place, businesses should continuously monitor its performance and make adjustments as needed. Key performance indicators (KPIs) related to customer satisfaction, supplier performance, inventory levels, and order fulfillment should be tracked regularly. Feedback from both customers and suppliers should also be gathered to identify areas for improvement. By continuously monitoring and refining the system, businesses can ensure that their approach remains effective and aligned with evolving market conditions.

Conclusion

A unified approach to Customer Relationship Management and Supplier Relationship Management is no longer a luxury but a necessity for businesses seeking to thrive in a competitive, customer-driven marketplace. By bridging the divide between customer and supplier relationships, organizations can enhance communication, improve forecasting, streamline processes, and create stronger partnerships. This integration not only helps businesses provide better customer experiences but also ensures that their supply chains are more resilient, adaptive, and efficient.

As businesses continue to navigate the complexities of global supply chains and ever-changing customer expectations, a unified relationship management strategy will be a critical factor in achieving long-term success. Through careful planning, technology adoption, and a focus on collaboration, companies can integrate CRM and SRM to create a seamless, holistic approach that drives growth and competitive advantage.

17. Data Integration Across CRM and SRM: Creating a Seamless Flow of Information

In today's competitive business landscape, organizations are constantly seeking ways to enhance their operational efficiency and build stronger relationships with both customers and suppliers. Central to achieving this goal is the seamless integration of Customer Relationship Management (CRM) and Supplier Relationship Management (SRM) systems. These systems, when working together, allow businesses to optimize both their customer and supplier networks, creating a more holistic and agile approach to managing relationships.

Data is at the heart of any CRM and SRM system, driving decision-making, forecasting, customer interactions, and supply chain management. However, when CRM and SRM are siloed, data often becomes fragmented and disconnected, hindering communication and decision-making. Integrating data from both CRM and SRM systems provides a unified view of an organization's operations, enabling more accurate forecasting, improved customer service, and a more resilient supply chain.

This chapter explores the importance of data integration across CRM and SRM, the challenges businesses face, and the strategies and technologies they can employ to ensure a seamless flow of information. The integration of CRM and SRM data not only improves operational efficiency but also provides valuable insights that can drive growth and long-term success.

The Importance of Data Integration in CRM and SRM

Data integration is the process of combining data from various sources into a single, cohesive system. In the context of CRM and SRM, this means ensuring that data from customer interactions and supplier activities are linked and accessible across both systems. This integration is crucial because customers and suppliers are interdependent: customer demand influences supplier activity, and supplier performance impacts customer satisfaction. A seamless flow of information between CRM and SRM systems provides a comprehensive view of the entire value chain, allowing businesses to make informed decisions, anticipate changes, and respond to market dynamics more effectively.

By integrating CRM and SRM data, businesses can create a more synchronized approach to managing their relationships. For example, customer insights such as purchasing behavior, preferences, and feedback can be shared with suppliers to improve product offerings, streamline inventory management, and optimize delivery timelines. Similarly, data from suppliers, such as lead times, delivery schedules, and performance metrics, can be shared with customer service teams to provide better service and manage expectations. This mutual exchange of data helps both internal teams and external partners collaborate more efficiently and effectively.

Benefits of Seamless Data Flow Between CRM and SRM

The integration of data between CRM and SRM systems offers numerous benefits that enhance both operational efficiency and relationship management. These benefits include:

Improved Customer Experience

A seamless data flow between CRM and SRM enables businesses to better understand and serve their customers. By integrating customer data with supplier information, businesses can gain insights into how supplier performance affects customer satisfaction. For example, if a supplier is consistently late with deliveries, this may impact the customer experience. By sharing this data across both systems, businesses can take proactive measures to resolve issues before they impact customers. Furthermore, integrated data enables businesses to personalize their interactions with customers, providing more tailored solutions and offering products that align with customer preferences.

Enhanced Supplier Collaboration

With integrated data, businesses can share critical customer insights with suppliers to improve product offerings, streamline production processes, and better align with customer demand. Suppliers can be given access to relevant customer data, such as purchasing trends, product preferences, and seasonal demand patterns, which can help them anticipate future needs and optimize their operations. In turn, suppliers can provide businesses with more accurate delivery times, pricing information, and quality metrics, contributing to more efficient and collaborative relationships.

Streamlined Decision-Making

Data integration enables businesses to make more informed and timely decisions. By having access to real-time customer and supplier data in a single, unified system, decision-makers can quickly assess performance metrics, identify opportunities for improvement, and address potential issues before they escalate. For instance, integrated data can help businesses quickly identify if a drop in sales is due to supply chain disruptions or changes in customer preferences, allowing them to take corrective actions. Additionally, integrated data can improve forecasting accuracy by providing a more comprehensive view of both customer demand and supplier capacity.

Increased Operational Efficiency

The integration of CRM and SRM data reduces duplication of efforts, minimizes manual processes, and enhances overall operational efficiency. When customer and supplier data are stored in separate systems, employees must spend time manually transferring information, checking for discrepancies, and updating records. A unified data flow eliminates these redundant tasks, freeing up time for employees to focus on more strategic initiatives. Moreover, integrated systems allow for better coordination between departments, as sales, procurement, and customer service teams can all access the same data and collaborate more effectively.

Challenges in Data Integration Between CRM and SRM

While the benefits of data integration between CRM and SRM are clear, businesses often face several challenges when attempting to integrate these systems. These challenges can arise from technological limitations, organizational resistance, and data management issues.

Technological Challenges

Integrating CRM and SRM systems often requires the use of complex technologies and platforms that may not always be compatible. Many businesses rely on a mix of legacy systems, off-the-shelf software, and custom-built applications, making it difficult to achieve seamless integration. In some cases, businesses may need to invest in new software or develop custom APIs to connect their CRM and SRM systems. Additionally, integrating data from multiple systems may require significant time and resources to ensure data consistency and accuracy.

Data Quality and Consistency

One of the biggest challenges in data integration is ensuring the quality and consistency of the data. In many cases, CRM and SRM systems contain incomplete, outdated, or inaccurate data, which can lead to poor decision-making and operational inefficiencies. Before integrating data, businesses must clean and standardize their data, ensuring that it is accurate, consistent, and complete. This process can be time-consuming and may require the involvement of multiple teams, including data analysts and IT specialists.

Organizational Resistance

Integrating CRM and SRM systems often requires changes to existing workflows, processes, and team structures. Employees may be resistant to these changes, especially if they are unfamiliar with the new systems or fear that their roles will be impacted. Overcoming this resistance requires strong leadership, clear communication, and a commitment to training and support. Organizations must also ensure that the integration process is aligned with their overall business strategy and that employees understand the long-term benefits of the integration.

Strategies for Successful Data Integration

To overcome these challenges and successfully integrate CRM and SRM data, businesses must implement a well-defined strategy that addresses both technological and organizational considerations. The following strategies can help businesses ensure a smooth and effective integration process:

1. Invest in the Right Technology

Choosing the right technology is critical for successful data integration. Businesses should look for platforms that support data interoperability, such as cloud-based CRM and SRM systems that can easily integrate with other enterprise software. Additionally, companies should invest in data integration tools, such as middleware or application programming interfaces (APIs), that can facilitate seamless data exchange between systems. It is also essential to choose technologies that support data analytics, as this will enable businesses to derive actionable insights from the integrated data.

2. Standardize Data Formats

To ensure consistency across systems, businesses should establish data standards and guidelines that dictate how data is collected, stored, and shared. This may include defining standard data formats, naming conventions, and data fields. Standardizing data formats ensures that information is easily transferable between CRM and SRM systems and reduces the risk of errors or discrepancies. It also makes it easier to analyze data across systems and identify trends or patterns.

3. Ensure Data Quality

Before integrating data, businesses must ensure that the information in their CRM and SRM systems is accurate, up-to-date, and complete. Data cleaning and validation processes should be implemented to remove duplicate entries, correct errors, and fill in missing data. Regular data audits should be conducted to maintain data quality over time. By ensuring that the data is clean and reliable, businesses can avoid the risks associated with poor decision-making and operational inefficiencies.

4. Foster Cross-Functional Collaboration

Successful data integration requires close collaboration between IT, sales, procurement, and other key departments. Teams must work together to ensure that the integration process aligns with the organization's strategic goals and that all stakeholders are on board with the changes. Regular communication and collaboration throughout the integration process will help ensure that the project stays on track and that any issues are addressed in a timely manner.

5. Provide Training and Support

As organizations implement integrated CRM and SRM systems, employees must be properly trained to use the new tools and systems effectively. Comprehensive training programs should be developed to ensure that employees understand how to access and use integrated data, as well as how to adapt their workflows to the new systems. Ongoing support and troubleshooting should also be available to help employees overcome any challenges they encounter during the transition.

Conclusion

The integration of CRM and SRM data is essential for creating a seamless flow of information across the value chain, enhancing customer and supplier relationships, and optimizing decision-making. By breaking down the silos between customer and supplier data, businesses can gain a more comprehensive view of their operations and improve efficiency, collaboration, and forecasting.

While data integration presents challenges, the long-term benefits are undeniable. Through the right technology, data management practices, and cross-functional collaboration, businesses can create a unified system that supports better customer service, stronger supplier partnerships, and more informed strategic decisions. In a world where customer and supplier relationships are increasingly interconnected, data integration is a crucial enabler of business success.

18. Shared Metrics and Analytics: Measuring ROI on Relationships

In the modern business environment, measuring the return on investment (ROI) of relationships is no longer optional—it is essential for success. Both Customer Relationship Management (CRM) and Supplier Relationship Management (SRM) systems are integral to fostering long-term, mutually beneficial relationships. However, without clear metrics and analytics, organizations are unable to accurately measure the effectiveness of these relationships, leading to missed opportunities, inefficiencies, and a lack of insight into areas for improvement.

The concept of shared metrics and analytics refers to the practice of aligning performance indicators and analytical tools across both customer and supplier relationships to provide a unified view of the business's performance. By establishing shared metrics that are relevant to both CRM and SRM, organizations can track, analyze, and optimize their relationships with customers and suppliers in a way that drives growth, efficiency, and strategic alignment. This integrated approach allows companies to measure the collective impact of CRM and SRM efforts, identify areas of overlap, and optimize resource allocation to drive greater value across the entire value chain. The ultimate goal is to create a set of shared metrics that can provide a holistic view of business performance, with a focus on long-term, sustainable growth rather than short-term transactional success.

Understanding the Importance of Measuring ROI on Relationships

The ability to quantify the return on investment for both customer and supplier relationships is critical to determining whether the resources invested in managing these relationships are yielding positive results. For CRM, ROI is often measured in terms of customer lifetime value (CLV), customer retention rates, and overall sales growth driven by loyal customers. For SRM, ROI is typically measured in terms of supplier performance, cost savings, risk mitigation, and innovation achieved through collaborative partnerships.

When both customer and supplier metrics are aligned, organizations can gain a comprehensive understanding of how well their relationship management strategies are working. This integrated approach allows companies to measure the collective impact of CRM and SRM efforts, identify areas of overlap, and optimize resource allocation to drive greater value across the entire value chain. The ultimate goal is to create a set of shared metrics that can provide a holistic view of business performance, with a focus on long-term, sustainable growth rather than short-term transactional success.

Defining Shared Metrics for CRM and SRM

To measure ROI across CRM and SRM, organizations must establish shared metrics that are relevant to both customer and supplier relationships. These metrics should reflect the strategic goals of the organization and provide a comprehensive picture of how both customer and supplier relationships contribute to business success. Some of the key shared metrics for CRM and SRM include:

Customer and Supplier Satisfaction

Customer satisfaction is a critical indicator of CRM success, while supplier satisfaction is equally important in SRM. By measuring satisfaction across both groups, organizations can gain valuable insights into the health of their relationships. For customers, satisfaction is typically measured through surveys, Net Promoter Scores (NPS), or customer feedback loops. For suppliers, satisfaction can be gauged through vendor assessments, communication quality, and responsiveness to issues.

Total Cost of Ownership (TCO)

TCO is a shared metric that applies to both customers and suppliers, measuring the total cost incurred over the lifecycle of a product or service. For CRM, TCO includes not only the purchase price but also factors such as maintenance, service, and returns. For SRM, TCO can include procurement costs, transportation costs, and the cost of managing supplier relationships. By evaluating TCO across both customer and supplier relationships, businesses can identify opportunities to reduce costs and improve efficiency.

Collaboration and Innovation

Collaboration between customers and suppliers is a critical factor in creating value through innovation. By tracking joint initiatives, product development efforts, or problem-solving activities, businesses can measure the extent to which collaboration is driving innovation and creating new opportunities for growth. For CRM, this could be measured by the development of new product offerings based on customer feedback or co-creation efforts. For SRM, innovation could be measured by the introduction of new supply chain solutions, technology adoption, or process improvements resulting from supplier collaboration.

Time to Market

For both CRM and SRM, the ability to bring products or services to market quickly is a key indicator of operational efficiency. In CRM, time to market reflects how quickly a business can respond to customer needs and market demands. In SRM, time to market is affected by the speed at which suppliers can fulfill orders, innovate, and adapt to changes in customer demand. A shared metric for time to market allows businesses to track the efficiency of their entire value chain and identify opportunities for improvement.

Return on Investment (ROI) of Relationship Activities

ROI on relationship activities is perhaps the most direct shared metric, as it quantifies the financial value generated from investments in CRM and SRM efforts. For CRM, ROI is typically measured in terms of increased sales, higher customer retention, and improved profitability driven by customer loyalty. For SRM, ROI is measured through cost savings, improved supplier performance, and risk mitigation achieved through strong supplier partnerships. By measuring the ROI of both CRM and SRM activities, businesses can evaluate the financial effectiveness of their relationship management strategies and ensure that resources are being allocated efficiently.

Using Analytics to Drive Insights from Shared Metrics

While shared metrics are essential for measuring ROI on relationships, analytics is the key to unlocking actionable insights from this data. Advanced analytics allows businesses to go beyond basic reporting and identify patterns, correlations, and trends that can drive strategic decision-making. Analytics provides the context needed to understand the impact of customer and supplier relationships on business performance and helps organizations make informed decisions to optimize these relationships for long-term success.

Descriptive Analytics

Descriptive analytics focuses on summarizing historical data to understand past performance. By analyzing shared metrics such as customer satisfaction scores, supplier performance, or TCO, organizations can identify trends and patterns that indicate areas of strength or opportunities for improvement. For example, descriptive analytics could reveal that certain customer segments are more likely to provide positive feedback, or that specific suppliers consistently outperform others in terms of delivery times and product quality. This insight allows businesses to make data-driven decisions to improve both customer and supplier relationships.

Predictive Analytics

Predictive analytics goes a step further by using historical data to forecast future outcomes. By analyzing shared metrics across CRM and SRM, businesses can predict customer behavior, demand fluctuations, and potential supplier disruptions. For example, predictive models can be used to forecast customer churn, identify at-risk suppliers, or predict demand spikes for specific products. Armed with these insights, businesses can take proactive steps to mitigate risks, enhance customer experiences, and strengthen supplier partnerships before issues arise.

Prescriptive Analytics

Prescriptive analytics provides actionable recommendations based on data-driven insights. By leveraging shared metrics and advanced analytics, organizations can receive guidance on how to optimize their relationships with both customers and suppliers. For example, prescriptive analytics could recommend which suppliers to prioritize based on performance data or suggest personalized offers for high-value customers based on purchasing behavior. This type of analytics helps businesses take specific actions to drive continuous improvement in their CRM and SRM efforts.

Tools and Technologies for Measuring Shared Metrics and Analytics

The implementation of shared metrics and analytics requires the use of advanced tools and technologies that can integrate data from both CRM and SRM systems and provide actionable insights. Some of the key tools and technologies that facilitate the measurement and analysis of shared metrics include:

Customer Relationship Management (CRM) Software

Modern CRM systems provide a wealth of data on customer interactions, preferences, and behaviors. By integrating shared metrics into CRM platforms, businesses can track customer satisfaction, ROI on relationship activities, and time to market. Many CRM systems also offer built-in analytics features that allow businesses to analyze customer data and generate reports on performance.

Supplier Relationship Management (SRM) Software

SRM systems help businesses manage their supplier relationships by providing insights into supplier performance, collaboration efforts, and costs. These systems can integrate shared metrics such as TCO, supplier satisfaction, and ROI on relationship activities. SRM software also often includes analytics capabilities to help businesses identify trends and opportunities for improvement.

Business Intelligence (BI) Tools

Business intelligence tools such as Tableau, Power BI, and Qlik allow businesses to integrate data from both CRM and SRM systems and create custom dashboards and reports. These tools enable advanced analytics, such as predictive and prescriptive analysis, and provide real-time insights into shared metrics across the value chain. BI tools help organizations visualize data, track performance, and make data-driven decisions that optimize both customer and supplier relationships.

Conclusion

Measuring the ROI of relationships is critical for businesses looking to optimize their CRM and SRM efforts and drive sustainable growth. By establishing shared metrics and leveraging advanced analytics, businesses can gain a holistic view of how their customer and supplier relationships contribute to overall performance. Through the use of descriptive, predictive, and prescriptive analytics, organizations can identify areas for improvement, optimize resource allocation, and make informed decisions that drive greater value across the value chain. The integration of shared metrics and analytics not only enhances the measurement of ROI but also provides actionable insights that support long-term success in an increasingly interconnected business environment.

19. Overcoming Integration Challenges: Aligning Processes, Tools, and Culture

In today's competitive and fast-paced business environment, organizations increasingly recognize the importance of effective integration between their customer relationship management (CRM) and supplier relationship management (SRM) systems. While both CRM and SRM systems play distinct roles in managing external relationships, integrating them effectively can provide businesses with a more comprehensive view of their operations, streamline workflows, and ultimately drive better decision-making. However, achieving successful integration between CRM and SRM is far from straightforward. Organizations often encounter a variety of challenges in aligning processes, tools, and culture, all of which can hinder the ability to fully capitalize on the potential benefits of integration.

The integration of CRM and SRM is not just a technological exercise but requires a holistic approach that addresses people, processes, and systems. Overcoming these integration challenges requires a careful balance between aligning organizational processes, ensuring compatibility between technology platforms, and fostering a culture that supports collaboration and data sharing. Without overcoming these obstacles, businesses risk losing out on the strategic advantages that a unified approach to relationship management can bring.

Aligning Processes Across CRM and SRM

One of the primary challenges in integrating CRM and SRM is aligning the processes used in each system. CRM and SRM systems typically operate with distinct sets of processes that focus on different stages of the customer and supplier lifecycle. CRM processes are often geared toward managing customer acquisition, retention, and loyalty, while SRM processes focus on sourcing, procurement, and supplier collaboration. These differing processes can result in silos within the organization, where data and workflows related to customer and supplier relationships are managed separately.

Aligning these processes requires an understanding of the overlaps between CRM and SRM activities and a willingness to redesign workflows that integrate both. A key challenge lies in ensuring that processes are flexible enough to accommodate the different needs of customers and suppliers while still maintaining alignment between the two. For example, customer data gathered through CRM systems may need to be shared with suppliers in SRM systems for purposes such as demand forecasting or inventory planning. In turn, supplier performance data collected in SRM systems may inform customer relationship strategies in CRM systems, such as determining the best suppliers for specific customer segments.

To overcome process alignment challenges, organizations should focus on creating shared workflows that are adaptable to both CRM and SRM needs. This requires a clear understanding of how customer and supplier interactions impact one another and the ability to design processes that facilitate collaboration and data sharing across departments. Additionally, organizations must ensure that processes remain streamlined and efficient, with a clear focus on reducing duplication of efforts and improving responsiveness to both customers and suppliers.

Selecting the Right Tools for Integration

Another significant challenge in overcoming integration barriers lies in selecting the right tools and technologies that can seamlessly integrate CRM and SRM systems. Businesses often use separate software solutions for CRM and SRM, and these systems may be incompatible with one another, requiring significant customization or manual data entry to align them. This lack of integration can result in data inconsistencies, inefficiencies, and missed opportunities for collaboration.

The key to addressing this challenge lies in selecting tools and platforms that offer strong integration capabilities. Many modern CRM and SRM systems come with built-in integration features that allow businesses to connect their systems with minimal effort. However, even with these integration features, organizations must ensure that the tools they choose are compatible with existing enterprise resource planning (ERP) systems and other business tools, such as marketing automation or supply chain management software.

A crucial consideration when selecting CRM and SRM tools is ensuring that they support the same data standards and formats. Data integrity is vital for successful integration, as misaligned or inconsistent data can lead to inaccurate decision-making. Organizations should prioritize solutions that offer robust data mapping and transformation capabilities to ensure a seamless flow of information between CRM and SRM systems. Additionally, businesses should also explore the potential for using application programming interfaces (APIs) and middleware platforms to bridge gaps between different systems and create a more integrated technology ecosystem.

Finally, it is essential for businesses to assess the scalability of their chosen tools. As organizations grow and evolve, their CRM and SRM needs will likely change as well. Choosing flexible and scalable tools will ensure that integration remains effective over time and can accommodate future business needs, whether in terms of expanding customer bases or diversifying supplier networks.

Cultivating a Collaborative Culture

Perhaps one of the most challenging aspects of integrating CRM and SRM is fostering a culture that supports collaboration between teams that manage customer and supplier relationships. In many organizations, CRM and SRM are managed by separate departments or teams that may not always share the same goals or priorities. For example, the sales and marketing teams responsible for CRM often prioritize customer acquisition and retention, while procurement and supply chain teams managing SRM focus on optimizing supplier performance and cost efficiency.

This siloed approach can create friction between departments and hinder the integration of CRM and SRM systems. To overcome this challenge, organizations must cultivate a culture of collaboration that encourages cross-functional teamwork and data sharing. This can be achieved through the establishment of shared goals, joint performance metrics, and regular communication between CRM and SRM teams. Additionally, organizations can encourage collaboration through the use of shared platforms and tools that allow employees from different departments to work together more effectively.

Leadership plays a crucial role in fostering this collaborative culture. Executives and managers must communicate the strategic importance of integrating CRM and SRM systems and provide the necessary support to ensure that the integration process is successful. This includes not only investing in the right tools and technologies but also ensuring that employees have the training and resources they need to work across functions effectively.

Another important aspect of creating a collaborative culture is promoting a customer-centric mindset throughout the organization. By recognizing that both customers and suppliers are integral to the success of the business, organizations can align their teams around a common objective: to create value for both customers and suppliers. This shift in mindset helps to break down traditional silos and encourages employees to view CRM and SRM as complementary functions rather than separate, isolated systems.

Overcoming Resistance to Change

Integration efforts often face resistance from employees who are accustomed to existing processes and systems. Employees may be reluctant to adopt new technologies, change their workflows, or work with colleagues from other departments. Overcoming this resistance requires effective change management strategies that involve clear communication, employee engagement, and training.

Leaders must communicate the benefits of integration in a way that resonates with employees. By emphasizing how the integration of CRM and SRM will improve business outcomes, reduce inefficiencies, and create a more seamless working environment, employees are more likely to embrace the changes. Additionally, involving employees early in the integration process and seeking their input can help build buy-in and mitigate resistance.

Training is another critical element in overcoming resistance. Providing comprehensive training on the new processes, tools, and systems will ensure that employees feel confident in using the integrated CRM and SRM platforms. This also helps to prevent frustration or confusion that may arise from unfamiliar systems, leading to smoother adoption and greater overall success.

Managing Data and Information Flow

Data management is a critical aspect of integrating CRM and SRM systems. The seamless flow of accurate, timely information between systems is essential for decision-making, collaboration, and overall business success. However, managing data across CRM and SRM platforms can be challenging due to differences in data formats, structures, and storage locations.

To overcome this challenge, businesses must implement strong data governance practices that ensure data consistency and integrity across both CRM and SRM systems. This includes creating standardized data formats, regular data validation processes, and clear protocols for data entry and maintenance. Organizations should also prioritize data security to protect sensitive customer and supplier information.

Advanced data integration tools, such as middleware and data warehouses, can help streamline the data management process by providing a centralized repository for information from both CRM and SRM systems. These tools enable businesses to automate data synchronization, reduce manual data entry, and ensure that data is always up-to-date and accurate across all systems.

Conclusion

Integrating CRM and SRM systems is a complex and multifaceted process that requires careful attention to aligning processes, selecting the right tools, fostering a collaborative culture, and overcoming resistance to change. By addressing these challenges head-on and adopting a strategic, holistic approach to integration, organizations can unlock the full potential of their customer and supplier relationships. Ultimately, successful CRM and SRM integration leads to improved operational efficiency, enhanced decision-making, and a more cohesive business strategy that drives long-term growth and success. Overcoming integration challenges may take time and effort, but the rewards—both in terms of business performance and relationship management—are well worth the investment.

20. Collaborative Case Studies: Examples of Successful CRM-SRM Integration

The integration of Customer Relationship Management (CRM) and Supplier Relationship Management (SRM) systems has become an essential strategy for businesses looking to enhance collaboration, streamline operations, and improve customer and supplier engagement. However, achieving this integration is no small feat. It requires careful planning, coordination, and a strategic approach to both technology and processes. In this chapter, we will explore several case studies from various industries where CRM-SRM integration has been successfully implemented, shedding light on the challenges faced, solutions applied, and the outcomes achieved. These case studies will provide valuable insights for organizations seeking to integrate these critical systems and foster a more collaborative and efficient business environment.

Case Study 1: A Global Electronics Manufacturer

A leading global electronics manufacturer with a vast network of suppliers and customers recognized the need to integrate its CRM and SRM systems to improve supply chain management, enhance customer satisfaction, and drive innovation. The company had been using separate CRM and SRM platforms, with customer-facing teams using CRM to manage sales, marketing, and customer service, while the procurement and logistics teams relied on SRM to manage supplier relationships, procurement processes, and inventory.

Challenges

The company faced several challenges in managing customer and supplier interactions separately. Data was often siloed, making it difficult for different teams to access and share insights. For example, sales teams lacked real-time data on supplier performance, while procurement teams had limited visibility into customer demand and preferences. This led to inefficiencies in forecasting, order fulfillment, and inventory management. Additionally, there was a lack of communication between the CRM and SRM teams, which hindered the ability to respond quickly to customer needs and supplier issues.

Solution

The company implemented an integrated CRM-SRM platform that combined data from both systems, allowing for real-time visibility into customer and supplier interactions. The new platform enabled customer service teams to view order histories, customer preferences, and supplier performance metrics, while procurement teams gained insights into customer demand trends and sales forecasts. This integration was facilitated by a cloud-based platform that connected all relevant teams and stakeholders.

To support the integration, the company standardized its data management practices and introduced automated workflows that allowed for seamless communication between departments. For example, when a customer placed an order, the sales team's CRM system would automatically send order details to the procurement team's SRM system, triggering the necessary actions to fulfill the order. The procurement team, in turn, could track supplier performance and make adjustments to ensure timely delivery and product quality.

Outcome

The CRM-SRM integration significantly improved operational efficiency and responsiveness. The company was able to reduce lead times by improving inventory management and optimizing procurement processes. With better visibility into customer demand and supplier performance, the company could align its supply chain more effectively, ensuring that the right products were available at the right time. This also led to higher levels of customer satisfaction, as the company could fulfill orders more accurately and promptly. Additionally, the integration allowed for better supplier collaboration, leading to cost savings and improved product innovation.

Case Study 2: A Retail Apparel Brand

A well-known retail apparel brand operating in multiple regions struggled with fragmented customer and supplier data due to the lack of integration between its CRM and SRM systems. The company's CRM system managed customer profiles, sales interactions, and marketing campaigns, while its SRM system handled supplier communications, order management, and procurement. However, the lack of connection between the two systems made it difficult for the company to respond quickly to customer demand or coordinate effectively with suppliers.

Challenges

One of the primary challenges the company faced was the inability to forecast demand accurately. Marketing and sales teams relied on CRM data to understand customer preferences and sales trends, but they lacked visibility into supplier capacity and stock levels. On the other hand, the procurement team used the SRM system to monitor supplier lead times and inventory, but they were not aligned with customer demand data, leading to stockouts, excess inventory, and delays in fulfilling orders. The lack of a unified platform resulted in missed opportunities for cross-functional collaboration and limited communication between teams.

Solution

To address these issues, the company decided to integrate its CRM and SRM systems using an enterprise resource planning (ERP) platform that could connect customer data with supplier information. The new system allowed the marketing and sales teams to access real-time supplier information, including inventory levels, production schedules, and order statuses, while procurement teams could view customer demand forecasts, promotional activities, and sales trends. The integration also included automated alerts and notifications to ensure that both teams were aligned and could make adjustments as needed.

The company also implemented a shared analytics dashboard that provided insights into both customer and supplier performance. This dashboard allowed teams to track key metrics, such as order fulfillment rates, supplier delivery times, and customer satisfaction, all in one place. The shared dashboard helped bridge the communication gap between CRM and SRM teams, allowing them to collaborate more effectively on strategies to meet customer demand.

Outcome

The integration of CRM and SRM systems had a transformative impact on the company's operations. By aligning sales, marketing, and procurement teams, the company was able to improve its demand forecasting and inventory management, reducing stockouts and excess inventory. The integration also enabled the company to respond more quickly to changes in customer preferences and supplier performance, leading to faster product deliveries and improved customer satisfaction. Additionally, the shared analytics dashboard helped the company identify opportunities for cost savings, as procurement teams were able to negotiate better terms with suppliers based on real-time sales data.

Case Study 3: A Global Automotive Supplier

A global automotive supplier faced challenges in managing its complex supply chain and customer relationships due to the lack of integration between its CRM and SRM systems. The company served multiple industries, including automotive manufacturers, aftermarket parts suppliers, and fleet operators. Each of these customer segments had unique needs, and the company's procurement and supply chain teams had to manage relationships with a large network of suppliers to ensure timely delivery of high-quality parts.

Challenges

The company's CRM system primarily focused on managing relationships with automotive manufacturers, tracking sales interactions, and managing customer support, while its SRM system focused on managing the procurement process for raw materials and components from a diverse set of suppliers. Due to the lack of integration, the company struggled with fragmented data, making it difficult to respond to customer inquiries quickly or identify potential supply chain disruptions in a timely manner. Furthermore, the procurement team was often unable to anticipate changes in customer demand, leading to supply chain delays and missed production deadlines.

Solution

To address these challenges, the company implemented a hybrid solution that integrated both its CRM and SRM systems into a unified platform, allowing real-time data sharing between sales, customer support, and procurement teams. The new platform provided a centralized database that stored customer profiles, sales histories, supplier performance data, and inventory levels. By integrating these systems, the company gained a more holistic view of both its customer needs and supplier capabilities.

The company also implemented predictive analytics tools that used historical data to forecast customer demand and identify potential supply chain risks. This allowed the procurement team to adjust production schedules and collaborate with suppliers more effectively. Additionally, the platform featured automated workflows that facilitated communication between departments and suppliers, ensuring that customer requirements were met promptly.

Outcome

The integration of CRM and SRM systems resulted in significant improvements in operational efficiency, customer satisfaction, and supplier collaboration. The company was able to reduce lead times by aligning production schedules with customer demand, leading to faster deliveries and better service levels. The predictive analytics tools enabled the company to anticipate customer needs more accurately, reducing the risk of overstocking or stockouts. Additionally, the integration allowed for better supplier performance tracking, leading to stronger partnerships and more efficient procurement processes.

Conclusion

These case studies highlight the transformative power of CRM-SRM integration in different industries. Whether it's a global electronics manufacturer, a retail apparel brand, or an automotive supplier, the integration of CRM and SRM systems enables organizations to better align their customer and supplier relationships, streamline workflows, and improve decision-making. The successful integration of CRM and

SRM leads to enhanced visibility, collaboration, and efficiency across departments, allowing businesses to respond more quickly to market changes, optimize their supply chains, and deliver superior customer experiences.

For organizations seeking to replicate these successes, it is essential to approach CRM-SRM integration with a strategic mindset that considers both technological and organizational factors. By overcoming the challenges of process alignment, data integration, and cross-functional collaboration, businesses can unlock the full potential of their CRM and SRM systems and achieve sustainable growth in an increasingly competitive marketplace.

Part 5: Advanced Strategies and the Future of CRM and SRM

21. AI and Machine Learning in CRM and SRM: Enhancing Decision-Making and Predictions

In today's fast-paced and highly competitive business landscape, both Customer Relationship Management (CRM) and Supplier Relationship Management (SRM) are critical pillars that support the growth and efficiency of organizations. However, to remain relevant and thrive, businesses must continually evolve their practices, leveraging advanced technologies to enhance decision-making, streamline operations, and better predict future trends. Among these technologies, Artificial Intelligence (AI) and Machine Learning (ML) are gaining significant traction as transformative forces in CRM and SRM strategies. This chapter will explore how AI and ML are being used in both CRM and SRM to optimize decision-making, improve predictive capabilities, and ultimately drive business success.

Understanding AI and ML in the Context of CRM and SRM

Before delving into the application of AI and ML in CRM and SRM, it is important to first understand what these technologies are and how they work in the context of business management.

Artificial Intelligence (AI) refers to the capability of machines to perform tasks that typically require human intelligence. These tasks include problem-solving, pattern recognition, and learning from past experiences to improve future performance. AI can process vast amounts of data much faster and more accurately than humans, making it a powerful tool for both CRM and SRM.

Machine Learning (ML) is a subset of AI that focuses on the ability of systems to learn from data, improve over time, and make decisions with minimal human intervention. ML algorithms can analyze historical data, identify patterns, and predict future outcomes, making it highly valuable for decision-making in both customer and supplier relationship management.

In CRM, AI and ML can help companies understand customer preferences, predict customer behaviors, and personalize interactions at scale. In SRM, these technologies can assist in predicting supplier performance, optimizing procurement processes, and mitigating risks in the supply chain.

The Role of AI and ML in CRM

The application of AI and ML in CRM is enabling companies to create more personalized, data-driven, and customer-centric strategies. Below are several key areas where AI and ML are being applied:

Predicting Customer Behavior

AI and ML models are highly effective at analyzing customer behavior. By evaluating past purchasing patterns, browsing habits, and interactions with marketing campaigns, these systems can predict future behavior with remarkable accuracy. For instance, AI-powered tools can forecast which customers are likely to make repeat purchases, when they might be ready to buy again, or which products they might be interested in. This predictive capability allows businesses to tailor their marketing efforts and sales strategies more effectively, driving higher conversion rates and improving customer satisfaction.

Personalizing Customer Interactions

One of the most significant advantages of AI in CRM is its ability to deliver personalized customer experiences at scale. Through machine learning algorithms, businesses can analyze customer data in real-time, enabling them to offer personalized recommendations, targeted marketing messages, and customized support. For example, an e-commerce company can use AI to recommend products based on a customer's previous purchases or browsing history, creating a more relevant and engaging experience. The ability to deliver hyper-personalized content improves customer loyalty and enhances the overall brand experience.

Enhancing Customer Service with Chatbots and Virtual Assistants

AI-powered chatbots and virtual assistants are revolutionizing customer service in CRM. These tools can handle customer inquiries, resolve issues, and provide 24/7 support without human intervention. Chatbots leverage natural language processing (NLP) to understand and respond to customer queries, while virtual assistants go a step further by proactively offering solutions, reminders, and support based on customer data and behavior patterns. As a result, businesses can reduce response times, improve service levels, and enhance customer satisfaction while lowering operational costs.

Optimizing Marketing Campaigns

AI and ML play a pivotal role in optimizing marketing campaigns by providing deep insights into customer preferences and behaviors. These technologies can identify which marketing channels are most effective, what messaging resonates with customers, and when the best time to reach out is. By analyzing customer data from various touchpoints, AI systems can suggest content and offers that are more likely to drive engagement, leading to more effective campaigns and a higher return on investment (ROI).

Customer Churn Prediction

One of the major challenges in CRM is identifying customers who are at risk of leaving. Traditional methods of measuring customer loyalty, such as surveys or periodic check-ins, are often too slow or inaccurate. AI and ML, however, can predict churn by analyzing patterns in customer behavior, such as a decrease in purchase frequency or engagement with the brand. By identifying at-risk customers early, businesses can take proactive steps to retain them, such as offering incentives or personalized outreach.

The Role of AI and ML in SRM

Just as AI and ML have transformed CRM, they are also revolutionizing Supplier Relationship Management (SRM). Here's how these technologies are making a significant impact in supplier management:

Predicting Supplier Performance

In SRM, AI and ML can help predict supplier performance by analyzing historical data, such as delivery times, product quality, and order fulfillment rates. These insights enable companies to identify high-performing suppliers as well as those that may be at risk of failure. By forecasting supplier behavior, businesses can make more informed decisions when selecting and managing suppliers, leading to stronger relationships and more reliable supply chains. Predictive analytics also helps in anticipating potential disruptions, such as delays or quality issues, allowing businesses to take corrective actions before they affect operations.

Optimizing Procurement Decisions

AI and ML are also being applied to optimize procurement decisions. Machine learning algorithms can analyze vast amounts of data from various sources to recommend the best suppliers for specific products or services based on factors such as cost, delivery performance, and capacity. AI-powered systems can also help businesses optimize their procurement strategies by predicting the best times to place orders, negotiate prices, and manage inventory levels, ultimately reducing costs and increasing efficiency.

Automating Procurement Processes

AI and ML have the potential to automate many aspects of the procurement process, from supplier identification and selection to contract management and payment processing. For example, AI algorithms can scan supplier databases to identify potential candidates based on predefined criteria, while machine learning systems can monitor supplier performance in real-time and flag any discrepancies or potential issues. By automating routine tasks, businesses can free up valuable resources, allowing procurement teams to focus on more strategic activities.

Managing Supplier Risks

Managing supplier risks is one of the most crucial aspects of SRM. AI and ML can help mitigate risks by predicting disruptions, such as delays or supply shortages, based on factors like weather patterns, geopolitical events, or market trends. These predictive models can help businesses prepare for potential risks and take proactive measures, such as diversifying their supplier base or adjusting production schedules. AI can also monitor suppliers for compliance with ethical and regulatory standards, ensuring that businesses work with reliable and responsible partners.

Enhancing Collaboration and Communication

AI and ML can also facilitate better communication and collaboration between businesses and suppliers. By integrating AI-driven platforms that allow for real-time data sharing, businesses can keep suppliers informed of customer demand, inventory levels, and production schedules. Additionally, AI-powered collaboration tools can help suppliers optimize their own operations by providing them with insights into demand patterns, inventory needs, and order forecasts, ensuring a smoother, more synchronized supply chain.

The Future of AI and ML in CRM and SRM

Looking ahead, the role of AI and ML in CRM and SRM will continue to expand as businesses increasingly adopt these technologies to gain a competitive edge. In CRM, future advancements may include even more sophisticated predictive models, enabling businesses to anticipate customer behavior with unprecedented accuracy. AI-powered systems could also become more adept at understanding and responding to customer emotions, providing a truly personalized and empathetic customer experience.

In SRM, the future of AI and ML lies in the further automation of procurement and supplier management tasks, as well as in the development of more advanced risk management tools. Blockchain technology, when integrated with AI, could bring about even greater transparency and security in supply chain processes, allowing businesses to track and verify every step of the procurement process in real-time.

Moreover, as AI and ML evolve, they will enable more intelligent and adaptive systems that learn and improve from experience. This means that businesses will be able to leverage data-driven insights not only to optimize existing processes but also to uncover new opportunities for innovation and growth.

Conclusion

AI and Machine Learning are undeniably transforming both CRM and SRM practices, offering businesses a range of benefits from improved decision-making to more accurate predictions and automated processes. By adopting AI and ML technologies, companies can enhance their ability to understand customer behavior, predict supplier performance, optimize procurement strategies, and foster stronger relationships with both customers and suppliers.

As these technologies continue to evolve, businesses must remain adaptable, ensuring that they integrate AI and ML in a way that aligns with their organizational goals and enhances their overall strategy. The future of CRM and SRM will undoubtedly be shaped by the continued advancement of AI and ML, providing businesses with powerful tools to drive growth, innovation, and success in an increasingly competitive market.

22. The Role of Big Data: Driving Insights for Customer and Supplier Strategies

In the modern business environment, where information flows freely and rapidly, data has become one of the most valuable assets a company can possess. The vast amounts of data generated by customers, suppliers, and operations provide a wealth of insights that can drive business decisions and strategies. However, the true potential of this data can only be realized when organizations leverage it effectively. Big Data plays a pivotal role in transforming both Customer Relationship Management (CRM) and Supplier Relationship Management (SRM) by enabling businesses to derive actionable insights that inform decisions, optimize operations, and drive business growth. This chapter will explore the role of Big Data in CRM and SRM, examining how organizations can harness this resource to develop more personalized customer experiences, optimize supplier performance, and enhance overall business strategy.

Understanding Big Data in the Context of CRM and SRM

Big Data refers to the vast volume, velocity, and variety of data generated by businesses and individuals. It includes structured data (such as transactional records), semi-structured data (like social media posts), and unstructured data (such as customer reviews or call center transcripts). This data can come from multiple sources, including customer interactions, supplier transactions, social media, Internet of Things (IoT) devices, and even external sources like market trends and competitor activities.

Big Data analytics involves processing and analyzing this data using advanced algorithms and data models to uncover patterns, trends, and insights that are not immediately apparent. In both CRM and SRM, Big Data enables businesses to understand customer behavior, predict supplier performance, optimize operations, and drive strategic decisions based on real-time data.

The Role of Big Data in CRM

Customer relationship management is deeply rooted in the ability to understand customers' needs, preferences, and behaviors. Big Data empowers businesses to build a more detailed, dynamic, and actionable picture of their customer base, enabling them to deliver more personalized and responsive customer experiences.

Personalizing Customer Experiences

Big Data allows businesses to personalize interactions with customers by analyzing vast amounts of data from various touchpoints. By integrating data from customer profiles, social media interactions, transaction history, website visits, and more, companies can gain a holistic view of each customer. This data-driven understanding enables businesses to tailor product recommendations, offers, content, and services to individual preferences. For example, an online retailer can use Big Data analytics to suggest products based on a customer's browsing history, past purchases, and demographic information, resulting in a more personalized shopping experience that enhances customer loyalty and increases sales.

Customer Segmentation

Traditional customer segmentation often relied on basic demographic information, such as age, gender, or income. However, with Big Data, businesses can segment customers in more nuanced ways, based on behavior, interests, purchasing patterns, and even sentiment. Advanced analytics enable companies to create highly refined customer segments, which allows for more targeted and effective marketing efforts. For instance, an airline company might use Big Data to identify frequent travelers, those interested in specific destinations, or customers who respond well to particular types of promotions. This segmentation not only improves marketing effectiveness but also enhances customer retention by ensuring that communication is more relevant and timely.

Predicting Customer Behavior

One of the most powerful applications of Big Data in CRM is predictive analytics. By analyzing historical data, such as past purchasing behavior, interactions with customer service, and engagement with marketing campaigns, businesses can use predictive models to forecast future customer behavior. For example, businesses can predict which customers are most likely to churn, when they are likely to make their next purchase, or which products they are most likely to buy. This foresight enables companies to take proactive steps, such as offering special discounts or loyalty rewards to at-risk customers or preparing inventory for anticipated demand spikes.

Enhancing Customer Support

Big Data also plays a crucial role in improving customer support and service. By analyzing customer feedback, chat logs, and social media conversations, businesses can identify common issues, track sentiment, and address potential concerns before they escalate. Machine learning algorithms can be used to categorize customer service requests, flagging urgent issues or identifying common themes, allowing customer support teams to respond more efficiently and accurately. Additionally, predictive models can suggest solutions based on past interactions, reducing resolution times and improving customer satisfaction.

Real-Time Insights

Another advantage of Big Data is the ability to provide real-time insights into customer behaviors. Real-time analytics allow businesses to monitor customer interactions as they happen, enabling them to adjust strategies on the fly. For example, a business can use Big Data to monitor social media activity during a product launch, identifying customer concerns or trending topics in real time. This information can help companies respond swiftly to customer needs, manage brand reputation, and engage customers at the right moment.

The Role of Big Data in SRM

Supplier Relationship Management benefits greatly from Big Data analytics, as it helps organizations optimize procurement processes, improve supplier performance, and mitigate risks. Big Data enables businesses to analyze supplier data more thoroughly, leading to stronger supplier relationships and more efficient supply chain operations.

Evaluating Supplier Performance

Big Data allows businesses to analyze supplier performance from multiple angles, including delivery times, quality of goods, pricing, and reliability. By integrating data from procurement systems, supplier audits, and performance reviews, businesses can gain a more comprehensive view of supplier performance over time. This information helps organizations identify high-performing suppliers as well as those who may be underperforming. For example, a company might use Big Data to assess whether a supplier consistently delivers on time, provides products of the required quality, and adheres to agreed-upon terms. By tracking these metrics, businesses can make more informed decisions about which suppliers to continue working with, which ones to replace, and which ones to develop strategic partnerships with.

Predicting Supply Chain Disruptions

One of the critical applications of Big Data in SRM is the ability to predict and mitigate supply chain risks. By analyzing external data, such as weather patterns, geopolitical events, or economic conditions, alongside internal data from suppliers and logistics, businesses can predict potential disruptions. For instance, if Big Data analytics indicate a looming shortage of raw materials or disruptions in transportation due to adverse weather conditions, businesses can take steps to minimize the impact. This might involve sourcing from alternative suppliers, adjusting production schedules, or increasing inventory levels. By leveraging predictive analytics, companies can avoid costly delays and ensure continuity in their operations.

Optimizing Procurement Strategies

Big Data is instrumental in optimizing procurement strategies by providing organizations with deep insights into supplier pricing, contract performance, and market trends. By analyzing large datasets from suppliers, procurement teams can identify cost-saving opportunities, negotiate better deals, and optimize purchasing decisions. For example, Big Data analytics can reveal pricing trends across multiple suppliers, helping organizations identify the most cost-effective suppliers or negotiate better terms. Additionally, data-driven insights can help businesses optimize inventory management by predicting demand fluctuations and adjusting procurement strategies accordingly.

Strengthening Supplier Collaboration

Big Data can also enhance collaboration between businesses and their suppliers. By sharing relevant data and insights, companies can work more closely with their suppliers to optimize production schedules, streamline logistics, and improve product quality. For example, if a supplier has access to real-time sales data from a retailer, they can adjust production schedules to meet changing demand. By fostering data-driven collaboration, businesses can strengthen supplier relationships and improve supply chain efficiency.

Enhancing Risk Management

Managing supplier risks is a major concern for businesses, and Big Data plays a crucial role in identifying, assessing, and mitigating these risks. By analyzing data from various sources, such as financial reports, industry trends, and social media, businesses can gain insights into the financial stability, compliance status, and reputation of their suppliers. For example, predictive analytics can alert companies to suppliers that are at risk of financial failure or those that might be affected by regulatory changes. This early warning system allows businesses to take preventive actions, such as diversifying their supplier base or renegotiating contracts, to reduce exposure to risk.

The Future of Big Data in CRM and SRM

As technology continues to advance, the role of Big Data in CRM and SRM will only grow in importance. Businesses will increasingly rely on data analytics to drive decision-making, improve customer and supplier relationships, and enhance operational efficiency. The future of Big Data in CRM and SRM is likely to involve deeper integration with artificial intelligence and machine learning, creating more sophisticated models that can predict customer and supplier behavior with even greater accuracy.

Furthermore, as data privacy regulations become more stringent, businesses will need to be mindful of how they collect, store, and use data. Companies will need to balance the benefits of Big Data with the need to protect customer and supplier information and comply with data protection laws.

Conclusion

Big Data is a game-changer for both CRM and SRM. It enables businesses to gain deep insights into customer behavior, predict supplier performance, optimize procurement strategies, and mitigate risks in the supply chain. By harnessing the power of Big Data, companies can deliver more personalized customer experiences, make more informed supplier decisions, and enhance operational efficiency. As businesses continue to adopt data-driven strategies, the role of Big Data will only become more central to their success, helping them navigate the complexities of modern markets and maintain a competitive edge.

23. Global Trends in CRM and SRM: Adapting to an Interconnected World

In today's fast-paced, interconnected global economy, organizations face a complex and rapidly evolving business landscape. Technology has made the world smaller, and companies now operate across borders with increasing ease, interacting with customers, suppliers, and partners from around the globe. This new environment demands that businesses adapt their Customer Relationship Management (CRM) and Supplier Relationship Management (SRM) strategies to stay competitive and responsive to changes. The global trends influencing CRM and SRM are varied, but they share a common goal: to help businesses leverage technology, data, and partnerships in ways that drive growth, innovation, and sustainability. In this chapter, we will explore the key global trends shaping CRM and SRM and how businesses can adapt to these changes.

The Rise of Digital Transformation in CRM and SRM

One of the most significant global trends affecting CRM and SRM is digital transformation. Organizations across industries are increasingly embracing digital tools and platforms to enhance their customer and supplier interactions. From cloud-based CRM platforms that provide real-time insights into customer behavior to e-procurement systems that streamline supplier interactions, digital tools are revolutionizing the way businesses engage with customers and suppliers.

In CRM, digital transformation enables businesses to provide a more seamless, personalized, and integrated experience for their customers. Social media, email marketing, mobile apps, and chatbots allow companies to engage with customers in real time, gaining valuable feedback and fostering more meaningful relationships. The use of artificial intelligence (AI) and machine learning (ML) in CRM systems helps businesses predict customer needs and preferences, allowing them to deliver tailored experiences that drive customer loyalty and satisfaction.

In SRM, digital transformation has led to the rise of e-procurement platforms, cloud-based supplier management systems, and advanced analytics tools. These technologies help businesses streamline procurement processes, reduce costs, and build stronger relationships with suppliers. By using digital tools to monitor supplier performance, track deliveries, and manage contracts, companies can improve the efficiency and transparency of their supply chains, leading to stronger and more collaborative supplier partnerships.

The Increasing Importance of Data and Analytics

Data is one of the most valuable assets a company can possess, and this holds true for both CRM and SRM. As businesses collect ever-larger volumes of data from customers, suppliers, and operations, the ability to analyze and derive insights from this data has become crucial to success. This trend is particularly evident in CRM, where companies use customer data to better understand behavior, preferences, and purchasing patterns, enabling them to personalize interactions and improve customer satisfaction.

Advanced analytics and AI-driven insights are transforming CRM systems into powerful tools for predicting future customer behavior, identifying new sales opportunities, and improving retention rates. By leveraging data from multiple touchpoints—such as social media, website interactions, email campaigns, and sales transactions—businesses can create detailed customer profiles that allow for more targeted marketing, improved product recommendations, and more effective customer service.

In SRM, data and analytics play a crucial role in managing supplier performance, optimizing procurement strategies, and mitigating risks. By analyzing supplier data, businesses can identify potential issues with delivery, quality, or pricing before they become major problems. Predictive analytics can help companies anticipate disruptions in the supply chain, allowing them to take proactive measures to avoid costly delays or shortages. Additionally, data-driven insights enable businesses to assess the financial health and compliance of suppliers, reducing the risk of working with unreliable partners.

The Shift Toward Customer-Centric and Supplier-Centric Models

As businesses become more attuned to the needs of their customers and suppliers, there is a growing shift toward customer-centric and supplier-centric models. In CRM, this means focusing on delivering value to the customer at every touchpoint, from initial marketing efforts to post-purchase support. Rather than simply pushing products or services, organizations are working to understand the full customer journey and provide tailored experiences that foster loyalty and long-term relationships.

The customer-centric model emphasizes building deeper connections with customers by understanding their preferences, behaviors, and pain points. Businesses that embrace this model are using data and technology to create personalized experiences that address specific customer needs. For example, companies are leveraging AI and chatbots to provide instant support and personalized recommendations, improving customer engagement and satisfaction.

Similarly, in SRM, the supplier-centric model focuses on fostering long-term partnerships with suppliers, rather than viewing them as simply transactional entities. Businesses are recognizing the importance of collaborating with suppliers to drive innovation, reduce costs, and improve product quality. This shift has led to the rise of strategic sourcing, where companies work closely with suppliers to identify opportunities for mutual growth and create value beyond the basic exchange of goods and services.

In both CRM and SRM, the focus is shifting from short-term transactions to long-term relationships. By adopting a customer-centric or supplier-centric approach, businesses can create more sustainable, profitable partnerships that drive growth and success in the long run.

The Growth of Omnichannel Engagement

As customers and suppliers become more interconnected through digital channels, businesses are adopting omnichannel strategies to engage with them across multiple platforms. In CRM, omnichannel engagement refers to providing a seamless and consistent customer experience across a variety of touchpoints, including social media, mobile apps, websites, in-store experiences, and customer service channels.

Omnichannel CRM strategies enable businesses to meet customers where they are, whether they are browsing products online, interacting with customer service agents, or making purchases through a mobile app. By creating a unified view of the customer across all channels, businesses can offer more personalized and consistent experiences, improving customer satisfaction and loyalty.

Similarly, in SRM, omnichannel engagement is transforming the way companies interact with suppliers. Businesses are increasingly using digital platforms to communicate with suppliers in real time, track shipments, and manage inventory. Omnichannel SRM strategies also include using cloud-based systems and mobile apps to collaborate with suppliers on product development, quality assurance, and logistics. By enabling suppliers to access key information and collaborate more effectively, businesses can strengthen supplier relationships and improve overall supply chain performance.

Sustainability and Ethical Practices in CRM and SRM

As the world becomes more interconnected, there is growing pressure on businesses to adopt sustainable and ethical practices in their CRM and SRM strategies. Consumers are increasingly concerned about the environmental and social impact of the products and services they purchase, and they are more likely to engage with companies that prioritize sustainability and ethical business practices.

In CRM, businesses are responding to this trend by focusing on sustainability and transparency in their marketing and customer engagement efforts. Companies are using data to highlight their sustainability initiatives, whether it's promoting eco-friendly products, reducing waste, or supporting fair trade practices. Customers are increasingly seeking brands that align with their values, and businesses that can effectively communicate their commitment to sustainability are more likely to build strong, loyal customer bases.

In SRM, sustainability and ethics are also becoming critical considerations. Companies are seeking suppliers that share their commitment to sustainability and ethical practices. This has led to the rise of green supply chains, where businesses collaborate with suppliers to reduce their environmental impact, ensure fair labor practices, and promote social responsibility. Additionally, businesses are using data and analytics to track the sustainability performance of their suppliers, ensuring that they meet certain environmental and ethical standards. By promoting sustainability in their supplier relationships, businesses can improve their brand reputation and attract customers who prioritize ethical practices.

The Emergence of Blockchain Technology in CRM and SRM

Blockchain technology, known for its ability to provide secure, transparent, and tamper-proof records, is starting to make an impact in both CRM and SRM. In CRM, blockchain is being used to enhance data security and privacy, allowing customers to have more control over their personal information. With increasing concerns about data breaches and privacy violations, blockchain offers a decentralized way to store and manage customer data, giving customers more control over how their information is used and shared.

In SRM, blockchain is revolutionizing supply chain transparency and traceability. By using blockchain, businesses can track the origin of products, monitor supplier performance, and ensure the authenticity of goods. Blockchain technology provides a transparent and immutable record of every transaction in the supply chain, which can help businesses reduce fraud, verify product quality, and improve compliance with regulations. For example, a company could use blockchain to track the journey of raw materials from supplier to manufacturer, ensuring that they meet environmental and ethical standards at every stage.

Conclusion

The global business landscape is constantly evolving, and businesses must adapt their CRM and SRM strategies to thrive in this interconnected world. Digital transformation, data-driven decision-making, customer-centric and supplier-centric models, omnichannel engagement, sustainability, and blockchain technology are all driving change in CRM and SRM. By embracing these global trends, businesses can build stronger, more collaborative relationships with customers and suppliers, driving innovation, improving operational efficiency, and creating value for all stakeholders.

As technology continues to evolve, the role of CRM and SRM will become even more critical to business success. Companies that can leverage these trends to enhance their customer and supplier relationships will be better positioned to compete in an increasingly complex and competitive global marketplace. Adapting to these trends is not just a matter of survival; it is an opportunity to thrive in an interconnected world.

24. Preparing for the Future: Agility and Innovation in Relationship Management

In an increasingly fast-paced and dynamic business environment, organizations must evolve to stay ahead of the curve. The concept of agility and innovation in relationship management—whether in Customer Relationship Management (CRM) or Supplier Relationship Management (SRM)—is vital for long-term success. With the constant flux in customer demands, technological advancements, and global market shifts, companies that cannot adapt quickly will face significant challenges. This chapter explores how agility and innovation can serve as the backbone of successful relationship management, ensuring businesses remain competitive in an ever-changing world.

The Need for Agility in Relationship Management

Agility in relationship management refers to the ability of an organization to quickly adapt its strategies, processes, and tools in response to changes in the market, customer needs, or supplier conditions. In the past, companies often relied on rigid systems and long-term contracts that emphasized stability and predictability. However, today's business environment requires more flexibility, where the speed of response and adaptability to new challenges can determine a company's success or failure.

In CRM, agility allows businesses to quickly modify their strategies to meet the evolving expectations of customers. For example, customers today expect instant responses through various communication channels, including social media, email, or chatbots. If a company can't quickly adjust its communication systems to handle these requests efficiently, it risks losing customer trust and loyalty. Moreover, as customer preferences shift, organizations need to have agile systems in place that can capture these changes and adjust marketing or sales strategies in real-time.

For SRM, agility means being able to pivot and collaborate with suppliers quickly when unexpected disruptions occur—whether they are economic shifts, environmental crises, or political instability. Supply chains, especially global ones, are vulnerable to unforeseen events that can impact everything from raw material availability to delivery timelines. A supplier relationship management system that is agile can help companies react swiftly, find alternative suppliers, and ensure minimal disruption to operations. Additionally, agile SRM fosters a more collaborative relationship with suppliers, where both parties can address problems and innovate solutions rapidly.

Innovation in Relationship Management: Leveraging New Technologies

Innovation in CRM and SRM is increasingly tied to technological advancements. The fast pace of technological change—whether through AI, machine learning, data analytics, or blockchain—has opened up numerous opportunities for businesses to improve how they manage relationships with customers and suppliers. Companies that adopt innovative technologies are better equipped to deliver enhanced customer experiences, streamline operations, and make data-driven decisions.

In CRM, innovations in technology allow businesses to create personalized experiences for customers in ways that were previously impossible. The use of artificial intelligence (AI) enables businesses to predict customer behavior and personalize offers or recommendations with precision. Machine learning algorithms can analyze vast amounts of customer data, including purchasing history, browsing behavior, and social media interactions, to anticipate needs before they are even expressed. This allows companies to engage with customers in a way that feels intuitive and timely, strengthening the relationship and increasing customer loyalty.

For example, AI-powered chatbots are now being used to automate responses to customer queries, providing instant support 24/7. This not only improves the customer experience by reducing wait times, but it also allows businesses to collect valuable data on customer concerns, preferences, and issues. This data can then be used to refine marketing strategies or improve product offerings, all while strengthening the bond with the customer.

In SRM, innovation is reshaping supplier relationships through the use of blockchain technology, e-procurement systems, and advanced analytics. Blockchain offers transparency in supply chains, enabling businesses to track products from origin to delivery, verifying authenticity and compliance. This has significant implications for industries such as pharmaceuticals, luxury goods, and food, where traceability is crucial. By ensuring that all parties in the supply chain have access to real-time data, businesses can mitigate risks, reduce fraud, and increase trust between suppliers and manufacturers.

E-procurement systems, which automate procurement processes, are also enabling companies to innovate in their SRM strategies. These platforms provide real-time visibility into supplier performance, streamline purchasing processes, and reduce procurement costs. By integrating e-procurement systems with CRM platforms, businesses can foster deeper collaboration with suppliers, optimizing the supply chain while improving communication and relationship management.

The Role of Data in Driving Innovation and Agility

In the age of big data, the ability to capture, analyze, and act on data is central to both CRM and SRM innovation. For CRM, data provides invaluable insights into customer preferences, behavior, and sentiment, which businesses can use to tailor their offerings and improve their relationships with clients. A customer-centric approach powered by data allows companies to engage with customers on a more personal level, whether through targeted marketing campaigns, product recommendations, or personalized customer service.

By analyzing historical data, businesses can identify trends and predict future behaviors, enabling them to proactively address customer needs. For example, a retailer can use customer data to predict when a customer is likely to purchase a product again and send timely reminders or offers to encourage the purchase. Similarly, predictive analytics can help businesses anticipate customer churn and take steps to retain customers before they leave.

In SRM, data plays a critical role in supplier performance management, risk mitigation, and process optimization. By leveraging data analytics, companies can monitor supplier performance in real time, tracking key metrics such as delivery times, product quality, and compliance with contracts. This allows businesses to identify potential issues early and take corrective action before they affect operations. Furthermore, data-driven insights can help businesses identify opportunities for cost savings, process improvements, and innovation within their supply chains.

Integrating data across CRM and SRM systems creates a unified view of the customer and supplier experience, enabling businesses to make informed decisions that drive long-term success. By using data as the foundation for innovation and agility, companies can create more dynamic and responsive relationship management strategies that adapt to changes in both customer expectations and supply chain conditions.

Agility in Crisis Management

One of the key tests of agility is how well an organization can adapt during a crisis. Global events such as the COVID-19 pandemic, natural disasters, and geopolitical tensions have underscored the need for companies to have flexible systems and processes in place that can quickly adapt to disruptions.

In CRM, the pandemic forced many businesses to rapidly transition to digital platforms and remote interactions with customers. Companies that were already agile in their CRM strategies, with the infrastructure to support online sales and virtual customer service, were able to pivot quickly and continue serving their customers. Businesses that were less prepared struggled to maintain customer relationships, highlighting the importance of having agile CRM systems that can adapt to changing circumstances.

Similarly, in SRM, the COVID-19 crisis exposed vulnerabilities in global supply chains, forcing companies to quickly adjust their supplier networks. Agile SRM systems allowed businesses to rapidly find new suppliers, adjust procurement strategies, and shift to more localized sourcing. Companies that had previously developed strong relationships with suppliers were able to collaborate more effectively to navigate the challenges posed by supply chain disruptions, demonstrating the value of long-term, collaborative partnerships.

Preparing for the Future: A Roadmap to Agility and Innovation

To prepare for the future, organizations must take proactive steps to foster agility and innovation in both CRM and SRM. The first step is to invest in flexible, scalable systems that can easily integrate new technologies, adapt to changing market conditions, and respond quickly to customer and supplier needs. Cloud-based platforms, AI-driven analytics, and real-time communication tools are just some of the technologies that enable businesses to be more agile and responsive.

The next step is to develop a culture of innovation and continuous improvement. This involves fostering an organizational mindset that embraces change, encourages experimentation, and values new ideas. Businesses should invest in employee training and development to ensure that their teams are equipped with the skills needed to navigate new technologies and evolving customer and supplier expectations.

Finally, businesses must prioritize collaboration—both internally and externally. Agile CRM and SRM strategies rely on strong partnerships with customers and suppliers, and fostering collaboration is key to success. This means breaking down silos within the organization, encouraging cross-departmental collaboration, and working closely with suppliers to co-create value. By building a network of agile, innovative, and collaborative partners, businesses can position themselves for long-term success in an ever-changing world.

Conclusion

Agility and innovation are no longer optional for businesses that wish to succeed in the interconnected world of CRM and SRM. As technology continues to evolve, and customer and supplier expectations continue to shift, organizations must embrace these two qualities to stay competitive. By fostering agile systems, leveraging innovative technologies, and building a culture of continuous improvement, businesses can create relationships with customers and suppliers that are flexible, responsive, and mutually beneficial. Ultimately, organizations that can adapt quickly to change, embrace new technologies, and prioritize collaboration will be best positioned to thrive in the future.

25. Key Takeaways and Action Plan: Building a Sustainable Relationship Strategy

As organizations continue to evolve in an increasingly complex and interconnected business environment, building sustainable relationship strategies with both customers and suppliers is crucial to long-term success. The ability to manage and nurture these relationships with agility, innovation, and foresight is not just a competitive advantage but a necessity in today's fast-paced market. This chapter summarizes the key takeaways from the book and offers a practical action plan for organizations aiming to build and sustain successful relationship management strategies.

Key Takeaways

The importance of effective relationship management, both in the form of CRM (Customer Relationship Management) and SRM (Supplier Relationship Management), cannot be overstated. A sustainable relationship strategy goes beyond mere transactions and focuses on creating long-term value for both the customer and the supplier. Here are the core takeaways:

1. **The Power of Relationships**: Relationships are at the heart of modern business success. Strong, trust-based relationships with both customers and suppliers enable organizations to gain valuable insights, foster innovation, and achieve operational efficiency. Whether in CRM or SRM, a focus on long-term partnerships is key to growth.

2. **Agility as a Competitive Advantage**: In a world marked by constant change, agility is vital. Both CRM and SRM must be adaptable to shifts in market conditions, customer preferences, or supply chain dynamics. Organizations that can pivot quickly in response to disruptions, technological advancements, or new business opportunities will be best positioned to thrive.

3. **Innovation Drives Value Creation**: The integration of cutting-edge technologies such as AI, machine learning, big data analytics, and blockchain is transforming the way businesses interact with customers and suppliers. By leveraging

these technologies, businesses can gain deeper insights, improve decision-making, and create personalized experiences for customers while enhancing supplier collaboration.

4. **Data-Driven Decision Making**: The ability to capture and analyze data effectively is essential to understanding both customer and supplier behavior. Data-driven decision-making allows businesses to anticipate needs, predict outcomes, and personalize engagement, all of which are essential for long-term success in CRM and SRM.

5. **Collaboration is Key**: Successful relationship management requires collaboration—not only between customers and suppliers but also within the organization. Cross-functional teams, transparent communication, and shared goals ensure that CRM and SRM efforts are aligned and create value across the entire value chain.

6. **Sustainability and Ethical Practices**: With growing concerns about environmental impact, social responsibility, and ethical practices, sustainability has become a critical aspect of both CRM and SRM. Customers and suppliers alike are increasingly looking for partners that demonstrate a commitment to sustainable practices, making it essential for businesses to integrate sustainability into their relationship strategies.

7. **Risk Management**: In both CRM and SRM, effective risk management strategies are necessary to mitigate potential disruptions. Whether addressing customer dissatisfaction, supply chain interruptions, or external threats, a proactive approach to risk can protect relationships and ensure continuity in operations.

8. **Continuous Improvement**: The landscape of relationship management is constantly evolving. As customer expectations rise and supplier dynamics shift, businesses must continuously assess and improve their CRM and SRM strategies. This

involves regular feedback loops, performance tracking, and the willingness to adapt to new tools, technologies, and business practices.

9. **Unified Approach**: A successful relationship strategy integrates CRM and SRM. While these two disciplines are distinct, aligning them through shared metrics, data integration, and collaborative processes ensures a holistic approach to managing relationships across the value chain. By breaking down silos and fostering cooperation between the teams managing customers and suppliers, organizations can create a seamless, efficient, and mutually beneficial ecosystem.

Action Plan for Building a Sustainable Relationship Strategy

Building a sustainable relationship strategy requires a clear action plan that aligns business goals with the need for strong, agile, and innovative relationships with both customers and suppliers. The following steps outline a framework for organizations looking to implement and sustain such a strategy.

Step 1: Define Clear Relationship Objectives

The first step in building a sustainable relationship strategy is to clearly define the objectives for both CRM and SRM. For CRM, the focus might be on customer retention, satisfaction, and lifetime value, while for SRM, objectives might center around cost reduction, supply chain resilience, and innovation through supplier collaboration. It's crucial to align these objectives with the overall business strategy to ensure that relationship management efforts are contributing to broader organizational goals.

Step 2: Implement Agility in Processes and Tools

Agility should be embedded into every aspect of relationship management. This means selecting CRM and SRM tools that offer flexibility and scalability, as well as establishing processes that allow for rapid adaptation to changing customer needs or market disruptions.

Cloud-based platforms, real-time analytics, and AI-driven tools should be prioritized for their ability to provide instant insights and facilitate fast decision-making. In addition, organizations should foster a culture of agility by encouraging teams to embrace change and experiment with new approaches.

Step 3: Leverage Technology for Personalization and Innovation

Personalization is a cornerstone of modern CRM, and innovation plays a crucial role in SRM. Businesses should invest in technologies that enable them to create customized experiences for customers and to collaborate effectively with suppliers. AI, machine learning, and big data analytics are powerful tools that can be used to anticipate customer needs, improve supplier performance, and drive product or service innovation. These technologies should be integrated into the organization's relationship management systems to provide a seamless experience.

Step 4: Build Collaborative Partnerships

Both CRM and SRM should be based on collaboration rather than transaction. Building strong, long-term partnerships requires open communication, mutual trust, and a willingness to co-create value. For customers, this might involve engaging in two-way conversations, offering loyalty programs, and seeking regular feedback. For suppliers, collaboration may include sharing data, working on joint product development, or supporting each other in times of crisis. By fostering a culture of partnership, organizations can ensure that both customers and suppliers are invested in the long-term success of the relationship.

Step 5: Develop a Data-Driven Strategy

Data is at the core of a successful relationship strategy. Organizations should prioritize collecting, analyzing, and utilizing data to improve decision-making in CRM and SRM. This includes tracking customer behavior, measuring supplier performance, and using analytics to identify opportunities for improvement. A unified approach to data integration—where data from both CRM and SRM systems is shared and analyzed—ensures that businesses have a comprehensive view of their relationships across the value chain.

Step 6: Focus on Sustainability and Ethics

Sustainability is no longer a peripheral concern; it is a central pillar of relationship management. Organizations must integrate sustainability into their CRM and SRM strategies by ensuring that both customer and supplier relationships are built on ethical practices. This includes choosing suppliers that prioritize environmental responsibility, offering products that align with customer values, and demonstrating a commitment to social and environmental causes. Customers are increasingly making purchasing decisions based on these factors, and suppliers who align with sustainability goals are likely to become more strategic partners in the long term.

Step 7: Implement Risk Management Strategies

Risk management is a key component of any sustainable relationship strategy. In CRM, organizations should proactively address issues such as customer churn, dissatisfaction, or changing market dynamics. In SRM, risk management involves identifying vulnerabilities in the supply chain and developing contingency plans. Regular risk assessments, scenario planning, and proactive communication with both customers and suppliers are essential for mitigating disruptions and maintaining strong relationships during crises.

Step 8: Monitor and Measure Relationship Success

To ensure that relationship management efforts are paying off, businesses must regularly monitor and measure the success of their CRM and SRM strategies. Key performance indicators (KPIs) such as customer satisfaction, supplier performance, retention rates, and cost savings should be tracked and analyzed. Regular performance reviews and feedback loops allow organizations to identify areas for improvement and make adjustments as necessary.

Step 9: Foster a Culture of Continuous Improvement

Sustainability in relationship management requires ongoing effort. Businesses should foster a culture of continuous improvement by encouraging feedback from both customers and suppliers, tracking progress against goals, and iterating on relationship management strategies. This might involve investing in employee training, exploring new technologies, or refining internal processes. By consistently evaluating and improving CRM and SRM strategies, organizations can ensure that their relationships remain strong and effective over time.

Conclusion

Building a sustainable relationship strategy in both CRM and SRM is essential for thriving in today's interconnected and dynamic business world. By focusing on agility, innovation, collaboration, data-driven decision-making, and sustainability, businesses can create long-lasting relationships that provide value to both customers and suppliers. With a clear action plan and a commitment to continuous improvement, organizations can ensure that their relationship management efforts contribute to long-term success and resilience.

www.ingramcontent.com/pod-product-compliance
Lightning Source LLC
Chambersburg PA
CBHW071024240526
45469CB00006BD/2076